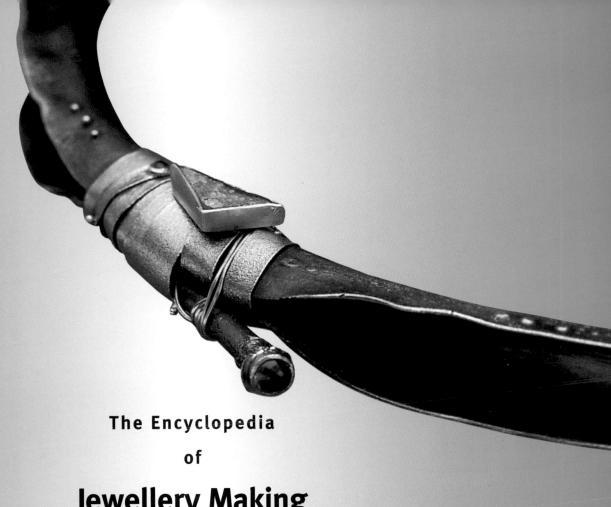

The Encyclopedia

of

Jewellery Making

Techniques

The Encyclopedia

of

Jewellery
Making
Techniques

Jinks McGrath

HEADLINE

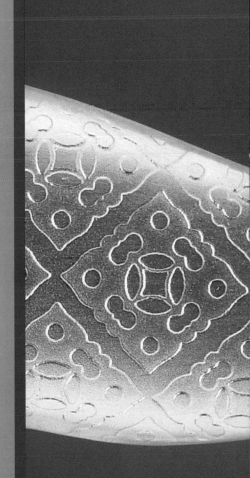

For Suzy and Tom
my favourite jewels

A QUARTO BOOK

Copyright © 1995 Quarto Publishing plc

First published in Great Britain in 1995 by HEADLINE BOOK PUBLISHING

British Library Cataloguing in Publication Data

McGrath, Jinks
    Encyclopedia of Jewellery Making Techniques
    I. Title

    ISBN 0-7472-1291-0

This book was designed and produced by
Quarto Publishing plc
The Old Brewery
6 Blundell Street
London N7 9BH

Editor Laura Washburn
Copy Editor Lydia Darbyshire
Art Editor Mark Stevens
Designers Nick Clark, Julie Francis
Diagrams Dave Kemp
Photographers Paul Forrester, Colin Bowling, Jon Wyand
Editorial Director Sophie Collins
Art Director Moira Clinch

Typeset by Central Southern Typesetters, Eastbourne
Manufactured in Singapore by Bright Arts (Singapore) Pte Ltd
Printed in Singapore by Star Standard Industries (Pte) Ltd, Singapore

HEADLINE BOOK PUBLISHING
A division of Hodder Headline PLC
338 Euston Road
London NW1 3BH

Publisher's Note
Jewellery making can be dangerous. Always follow the instructions carefully, and exercise caution. Follow the safety procedures accompanying the techniques.

As far as the methods and techniques mentioned in this book are concerned, all statements, information and advice given here are believed to be accurate. However, neither the author, copyright holder nor the publisher can accept any legal liability for errors or omissions.

6
Techniques

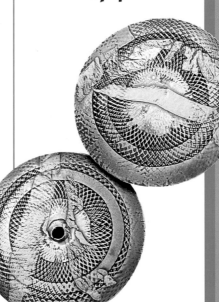

Contents

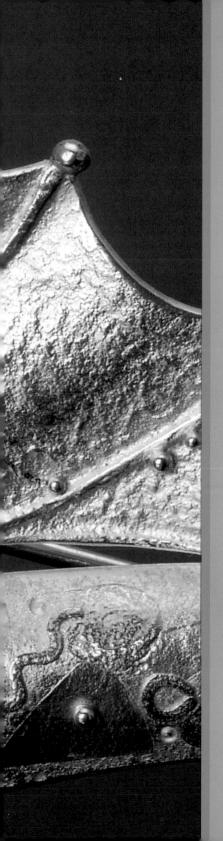

Techniques

THE FIRST SECTION OF THIS BOOK looks at the most often used jewellery making techniques. These techniques are arranged in alphabetical order, rather than in order of difficulty or in order of frequency of use. As you gain experience in working with metals and with using them in different ways, you will find that you use some techniques more often than others and you will learn how to use basic techniques in new ways to develop your work in unusual and individual directions.

There are, of course, different aspects and procedures within every technique, and in a book of this kind it has been impossible to cover every variation and permutation. Inevitably, there are gaps, and apologies if you encounter one. If a technique interests you, you should next turn to a more specialized text. Alternatively, experiment for yourself – experimentation is one of the most rewarding ways to discover how metal works and how you can use it.

You will find that several techniques – annealing, piercing and soldering among them – are essential to all stages of jewellery making, and you should master these basics before you try anything too elaborate. Where techniques are used in different procedures, cross-references will guide you to the relevant information.

Jewellery making is a rewarding and fascinating pastime. Although you may find that you enjoy some aspects of jewellery making more than others, the techniques described in this book will give you a thorough understanding of all the basic information you need to create unique and professional-looking pieces.

Basic Tools

When you are first beginning to work with jewellery, you will need only a few tools and pieces of equipment. Buy tools only as you need them. There is no need to acquire the full range when you are beginning.

Although it is possible to work in the kitchen, you should, if possible, try to have a special working area that can be either closed off or secured in some way, because some of the tools and pickles you will use could be dangerous in the wrong hands.

There is no need to buy a sophisticated work bench. An old table will suffice, as long as it is reasonably sturdy and does not wobble. Make sure that the table is a comfortable height. When you are working your elbows should be able to rest easily on the surface of the table, but try to keep your back straight while you work.

The wooden bench pin, which is the central working point, can be attached to the table with a C-clamp. Try to arrange the bench and working area so that the tools you use most often – pliers, snips and jeweler's saw, for example – are easily accessible. A hook or rack near to the bench pin is a neat and convenient method of keeping them near at hand. A small vise, which has

numerous uses, can be screwed to the edge of the table.

Make sure that you work under a good light. An adjustable table lamp is ideal, because the light can be directed to shine onto your work so that no shadows are cast. Bear in mind that when you are soldering and annealing you need to be able to turn off the light, so make sure that the switch is within easy reach. Protect the area of your bench or table that you use for soldering with a metal plate of some kind – an old roasting pan would be ideal – and stand the soldering block or charcoal block on the metal so that the surface of the bench is not damaged by the flame of the torch. Small soldering jobs can be done with a portable gas cylinder torch, but for everyday use, you will probably find a blow torch that uses propane gas and your own breath more than adequate.

Most polishing can be done by hand, especially at first. If

and when you do acquire a polishing motor, make sure that it has its own housing or that it has an integral dust extraction system. The dust created by polishing is dirty and gets everywhere.

The following tools and equipment are those you will need to get started. Buy other items as you need them so that you gradually acquire a fully equipped workshop.

Piercing saw This is the first tool to buy and the one you will keep forever. Buy the best you can afford. Blades, which are available in packs of 12, range in grade from 4/0, through 0, down to 0/6. To begin with, buy grade 1, 0 or 0/1.

Needle files It is possible to buy a packet of 8 or 10 useful

Basic tool kit
1 Parallel pliers; **2** small vice, suitable for fixing to the bench; **3** ring sizers; **4** stainless steel burnisher (should always be kept clean and polished); **5** round-nosed pliers; **6** snips; **7** hammer with a flat face and round nose; **8** hand-held ring vice; **9** stainless steel ring mandrel; **10** leather, placed beneath the pin on the bench to catch any filings and scrap pieces; **11** wax sheet, used for making casting molds; **12** sheets of brass and silver and silver wire; **13** pumice powder.

shapes. If you are buying individual tools, choose a flat, an oval, a half-round, and a triangular file to begin with.

Large flat file This tool is essential for removing lumps of excess solder, for straightening edges and for generally cleaning up your work. Make sure that it is not too coarse.

Large half-round file Use this for cleaning up the inside surfaces of rings and inside curves.

Ball pien hammer A general-purpose hammer has dozens of uses.

Round-nosed pliers These essential pliers are needed for bending curves, circles and wire.

Flat-nosed pliers These are used for holding, bending and forming. Buy two different sized pairs and make sure they are comfortable in your hand.

Half-round pliers These are useful for bending metal without marking the outside curve.

Serrated-edge pliers Although they will leave a mark when they are used for gripping metal, they are essential for pulling wire straight or through a draw plate.

Ring mandrel This tapered steel rod is used for shaping rings after soldering.

Wooden mallet Use this to shape and flatten silver. It will not leave marks on the metal.

Soldering torch Make sure that there is somewhere near the soldering area to keep the torch and that when it is in use the flame is always directed towards the soldering block.

Charcoal block Items that are to be soldered are placed on the block.

Borax dish and cone Flux is produced by rubbing the borax cone in a little water in the dish.

Binding wire Before soldering, hold two pieces of metal firmly together with wire. Always remove the wire before pickling.

Insulated tweezers Use tweezers to hold pieces for soldering or the solder itself when stick solder is being used.

Small vice Once it is firmly attached to the work bench, a vice will have dozens of uses, including holding formers, bending right angles, holding metal steady while it is being filed and holding draw plates.

Snips These are essential for cutting binding wire, paillons of solder, wire and even small pieces of metal.

Wet and dry papers Keep a good selection in stock, beginning with grade 240 and working through grades 400 and 600 down to grade 1200.

Safety pickle, alum or sulphuric pickle A pickle of some kind is needed to clean metal after soldering.

Liquid metal cleaner Ideal for polishing when the piece has been finished.

Leather or felt stick The final stage in polishing is buffing on a stick.

Water Wherever you work, make sure that you have easy access to running water.

Acrylics

Different kinds of acrylic materials can be used in jewellery to create light, crisp and colourful effects. You can make entire pieces from acrylic or it can be used in combination with metal in ingenious and subtle ways.

You can obtain acrylics from plastics suppliers, or you may live near to a company that makes small plastic articles and that would be happy to pass on off-cuts to you. If you buy it from a supplier you will be able to select from sheets, rods or tubes, circles, squares, rectangles and so on that are clear or coloured, transparent or opaque. It is an easy material to work with, because it can be cut by hand with a piercing or coping saw and it can be filed, polished, bent in gentle heat, drilled, carved or worked on a lathe.

Acrylic can also be used as a two-part resin, which is poured or "cast" into metal to give a finish that resembles enamel.

One problem with acrylic is that, compared with metal, it is very vulnerable, so its use needs to be carefully considered. The surface will scratch easily, and although the scratches can be easily removed, it is not always practicable to do so.

1 Sheet of frosted perspex;
2 epoxy resin; **3** large flat file;
4 coloured pigment which can be mixed into the resins to give colour.

Cutting

Acrylic or perspex sheets are usually supplied with a paper covering, and you can draw the pattern directly onto the paper before you cut out the design with a piercing or coping saw. You should use a no. 0 or no. 1 blade, or an even coarser one if necessary. Make sure that you catch all the dust and swarf from the acrylic in a clean bag below the bench pin because it is irritating to have acrylic mixed with the metal scrap. As it is cut, acrylic tends to get very hot, which makes swarf melt onto the piercing blade. Cutting slowly should overcome this problem, but if you notice that the acrylic is beginning to cling to the blade, clear it by drawing the edge of a file down each side of the blade.

Filing and finishing

Files can get clogged up quickly when they are used to smooth acrylics, and if you are going to use a lot of acrylics it is worth keeping a separate set of files. You will need a file brush to clean them regularly. Use the files in exactly the same way as you would on metal, removing the marks made by one file with the next size down. You can get a smooth finish by working through the various grades of wet and dry papers and then finishing off with a liquid metal cleaner. You can also use a polishing mop with grease-free white polish, which gives acrylic a shiny, clear surface. You must take care that it does not get too hot or the surface will start to melt and the polish will become a series of dragged black lines. Polish can be removed with detergent. Do not use acetone, turpentine, methylated spirits or benzene on acrylic because they can damage the surface.

An effective way of finishing polished acrylics is to deliberately make them frosty. This can be done with fine steel wool and detergent and water or with a brass brush, used

Cutting acrylics
Using an ordinary piercing saw or a coping saw to cut sheets of perspex.

Filing and finishing
File the edges with a suitably shaped file and polish with wet and dry papers, followed by liquid metal cleaner, applied with a cloth.

with detergent and held in the pendant motor. A satin or bark finishing brush can also be used on a polishing machine to give a frosty finish. Always wear safety glasses when you use these brushes because loose pieces of steel can fly off when they are in use.

Drilling and engraving
Most small holes can be drilled straight through an acrylic sheet or rod, but if you need to make a hole in a very thick sheet you will need to lift the drill in and out several times so that the acrylic does not get too hot and the swarf does not melt on the drill. The hole will be visible as a white line or, in transparent acrylic, as an opaque line.

Engraving tools can be used on acrylics but, again, the edges of the lines will be opaque unless they can be individually polished.

Casting
Mix the two parts of acrylic in equal proportions and add the appropriate colour. This mix can be poured into metal "cloisons" (compartments) or into a mould. You must pour the liquid resin steadily and slowly. If you pour too quickly heat can be generated and you may find that air bubbles appear. If you are pouring into metal cloisons the resin is usually poured so that it is a little higher than the edge of the metal. When it is hard, it can be filed level or rubbed down with wet and dry papers. Any holes that may have appeared after filing can be filled up and allowed to dry

before the piece is polished.

Pouring resin into a mould has to be done in two stages. First, the mould is half-filled and allowed to set before the other half is poured in. If you try to fill the mould at once, you will generate too much heat. You can take advantage of this natural break by changing the colour or even by introducing a small object.

Gluing
When you glue acrylic pieces together or to another material, you must use a clear, compatible adhesive. Some adhesives can be coloured with dye to match the acrylic.

Thermosetting
Thermosetting is a process whereby acrylics and plastics can be shaped by heat. This can be done in an ordinary domestic oven set at 175°C

(350°F/gas mark 4), over an electric hot plate or by using a blow torch. When the plastic has reached 175°C (350°F), remove it from the heat – you must wear thick, protective gloves – and use your hands to bend it round or into a mould. If you use a blow torch, use a gentle flame.

SEE ALSO

- Drilling 50–51
- Filing 68–70
- Polishing 104–105

Shaping acrylics
If it is heated gently, perspex sheet can be bent around a former or pressed into a mould.

Making a pair of lathe-turned acrylic earrings

1 Set the angle of cut on the lathe at 75 degrees and insert a round acrylic rod with a diameter of 15mm (⅝in) into the chuck. Carefully turn a cone shape.

2 Use the cutter to get as smooth a finish as possible. Use water or oil as a lubricant and work slowly up the acrylic, taking off no more than 0.2mm at a time.

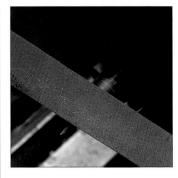

3 While the chuck is still rotating, smooth the cone still further with a single cut "dreadnought" file.

4 Use a parting-off tool, set at 90 degrees, to remove the cone from the rod. Make a second cone in exactly the same way.

5 Use wet and dry papers, grades 180 and 500, to smooth the acrylic even more, using the papers with water so that the work does not get too dusty. Next polish with a polishing motor with a muslin mop and grease-free polish or use a liquid metal cleaner and a rag. Polish off with a clean cloth and then wash in detergent.

6 The cones are now ready to be dyed.

9 When the fluid is dry, mix a second, darker colour in the same way as the first and place the cones in the dye.

10 When the cones are cool, peel off the masking fluid and drill a 0.8mm wide hole approximately 4mm (¼in) deep in the centre of the base of each cone.

7 Mix a small amount of dye powder in cold water in a small saucepan (check the manufacturer's instructions for precise quantities). Make sure that the mix is smooth then add a few drops each of the proprietary wetting agent and of the carrier. Add sufficient warm water to fill the saucepan and stir well before heating on an electric ring until it is nearly boiling. Place the cones in a metal sieve and lower them into the liquid. Do not allow the dye to boil or the acrylic will bend.

8 Take the cones from the dye from time to time to check the colour. A good depth should be achieved within a few minutes. Remove the sieve and wait for a moment or two for the acrylic to cool before rinsing and drying. Use a fine paintbrush to apply strips of art masking fluid. We painted five parallel lines on each cone.

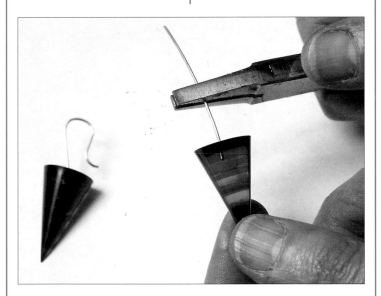

11 Use an impact adhesive or a two-part adhesive to glue silver wire, cut to about 40mm (1½in) long, in the hole. Use your pliers to bend the wire into shape.

Annealing

Annealing is the process used to soften metal by heating it before you begin to work with it. Metal is also annealed when it becomes "work hardened" – that is, when it becomes inflexible after being bent, drawn, hammered or beaten.

Each metal has its own melting point, and each metal, therefore, must be annealed at a different temperature. Some metals – fine (pure) gold and fine silver, for instance – need little or no annealing because they will remain pliable throughout most processes and can be reduced by up to 70 per cent before they require annealing. Other metals, especially copper, quickly become work hardened and need regular annealing.

Metal is usually annealed with a torch, and there are several types to choose from: air- or oxygen-assisted propane torches; mouth "blow" torches; propane gas torches; and natural gas torches. When you use a torch, a large "reducing" flame is played over the surface of the metal until it turns the right colour. The most effective part of the flame for annealing purposes is about 2.5cm (1in) or so from the end, at the point at which the orange centre meets the blue section.

Metals should be held at the correct temperature for about 30 seconds. It is, of course, impossible to measure the temperature of a piece of metal while it is being heated, but it is possible to estimate the temperature from the ways in which metals change colour as they become hot, and the ability to identify the different colours will come with time. It is easier to identify the colour of a piece of metal as it is being heated if the annealing is done on the dark area of a charcoal block. Draw the curtain to cut out any direct sunlight, and switch off your bench light when you are using a torch to anneal or solder.

Metal can also be annealed in a kiln, although by the time the kiln has warmed to the correct temperature it is usually quicker and more practical to use a hand-held torch. A kiln can be useful, however, if you are working with a large piece of metal or a coil of fine wire. It can, for example, be difficult to anneal wire with a gauge of 0.5mm or less because the wire could easily melt in the direct flame of a blow torch. Coil the fine wire into an old tin and place it in a preheated kiln for a minute or two.

The chart on this page indicates the different annealing and melting temperatures of the metals you will be working with. It also indicates how the metal should be cooled or quenched after annealing. These figures should be regarded as guidelines, and you should always check the technical data supplied by your metal dealer because they will always include precise instructions.

Annealing and Quenching Temperatures			
Metal	Annealing temperature	Melting temperature	Quench
Copper	600–700°C (1110–1290°F)	1080°C (1975°F)	Immediately
Silver	600–650°C (1110–1200°F)	890°C (1635°F)	Below 500°C (930°F)
Carat gold	650–750°C (1200–1380°F)	835–1000°C (1535–1830°F)	As indicated on technical data
White gold	650–750°C (1200–1380°F)	910–1315°C (1670–1400°F)	As indicated on technical data
Platinum	600–1000°C (1110–1830°F)	1755°C (3190°F)	Allow to cool in air then quench in water

1 Soldering block can be placed straight onto the bench with the charcoal block (**2**) on top.

❶

❷

SEE ALSO

• Pickling & quenching 98—99

Copper
1 Place the copper on a charcoal block.

Gold
1 Anneal 9 carat gold by heating the metal until it is a dull red. Hold it at that colour for a few seconds, then allow it to cool to black heat before quenching.

4 Anneal 18 carat white gold by heating it until it is deep pink. Hold it at that colour for a few seconds before quenching.

Silver
Place the silver on the charcoal block and heat with a large reducing flame until the metal is a dull pink. Hold the silver at that colour for a few seconds before quenching.

2 Heat the metal with a large reducing flame.

2 Heat 18 carat yellow gold until it is deep pink before quenching.

3 When the metal is a deep pink, extinguish the flame and quench the copper.

3 Heat 18 carat red gold until it is deep red. Hold it at that temperature for a few seconds before quenching.

Platinum
1 Heat the metal until it is a deep cherry red; allow to cool before quenching in water.

Anodizing

Anodizing was first used to wonderful effect in the early 1970s by such jewellers as Edward De Large and Brian Eburgh. Since then it has become a popular way of introducing vibrant colours into jewellery because the process is relatively inexpensive and quick to do. However, because the chemicals involved are so dangerous and because it is a fairly technical process, it is possible to send work to jewellers who specialize in the process to colour pieces professionally.

The process of anodizing the refractory metals titanium, niobium and tantalum produces a range of colours over the surface of the metal that is similar to the colours formed when oil floats on water. The effect is achieved by an electric current being passed through a solution to build up a layer of hard, transparent oxides on the metal. The thickness of the layer of oxides, which determines the colours that are seen, is determined by the relative area, time and voltage taken in the anodizing process.

The colours that are produced in this way are called diffraction colours, and the process works because each colour consists of a specific wave length of light. White light – that is, that carries all the colours – penetrates through the oxide layer and is refracted, reflected off the surface of the metal and then diffracted as it emerges through the oxide layer. In this way some elements of white light are cancelled out and some are amplified to produce particularly vibrant shades. The rougher the surface of the metal, the more intense is the colour that will be achieved. High voltage colours should be put on first because they do not need to be masked against the lower voltage colours. Apply a "stop out" resist, similar to that used in etching, to areas that need protecting against a higher voltage. It must be completely dry before the metal is immersed in the anodizing bath because "stop out" resists can lift off and peel away at very high voltages. It is possible to apply a coat of resist to a piece, to scratch a design or pattern through it and to anodize the metal at high voltage. You can then remove the varnish with a suitable solvent or turpentine and re-anodize the metal at a lower voltage. This process produces fine lines across the anodized colours.

Titanium can have patterns etched on it with hydrofluoric acid. Apply "stop-out" varnish to the areas you do not want to be etched before anodizing the piece. Another method is to wrap thin strips of masking tape in a random pattern around a piece of titanium. The anodized effect resembles bamboo stalks.

Tantalum and niobium anodize in the same way to titanium, and if the metals are combined and anodized at the same voltage different colours will be produced as they produce different colours at different voltages.

Anodized metal can be engraved or abraded and then re-anodized.

Tools and materials

The equipment needed for anodizing is specialized and technical. You will need: a variable transformer, capable of delivering from 3 to 120 volts at 1 amp; a non-glass container for the hydrofluoric acid; a glass vessel to hold a 50 per cent solution of lactic acid; a glass vessel to hold a solution of ammonium sulphate made in the proportions of 20g (1oz) to 1 litre (1¾ pints); plastic tweezers; titanium wires for the anode and cathode; strong rubber gloves. Protective goggles should be worn throughout the process.

SEE ALSO

- Etching & photoetching
64–67

Safety Procedures

The chemicals used in anodizing are dangerous. The most dangerous of all is hydrofluoric acid, which will cause serious burns if it comes in contact with your skin. Wounds caused by this acid ulcerate and do not heal. Hydrofluoric acid has to be kept in double-skinned plastic containers – it is used for etching glass – and it must always be kept in a locked cupboard, safely and securely away from children and animals. The other chemicals used in the process are lactic acid and ammonium sulphate.

If you carry out anodizing yourself, you must wear protective spectacles or goggles, heavy-duty gloves and an overall. Mix and use the chemicals out doors if possible; failing that make sure that you are working in a well-ventilated room.

Anodizing titanium
Etch the titanium by immersing it in a solution of 1 part hydrofluoric acid to 10 parts water for about 10 seconds. **Do this outside or in a very well-ventilated room.** When you cut the titanium leave a long, thin piece from one corner by which you can hold it and from which it can be wired to the anode.

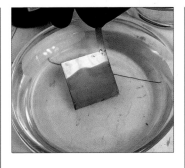

2 For the high-voltage colours (magenta, turquoise and green) you will have to use lactic acid. Transfer the titanium to the lactic acid to stabilize it. Electricity does not travel far in lactic acid, so work with the anode and cathode close. Both of these spark viciously when shorted and they blow fuses. It is therefore advisable to use ammonium sulphate.

4 The cathode wire is attached to a piece of stainless steel or to titanium.

5 Alternatively, use the metal end of a paintbrush as the cathode, and this can then be used to paint the surface of the titanium anode with the ammonium sulphate. Altering the voltage in the paintbrush (or cathode) will allow you to create some unusual colours.

1 Rinse the titanium well in water for 4–5 seconds. From here you have two choices: for normal anodizing proceed to step 3.

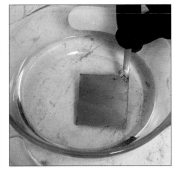

3 Rinse the piece in water again. Then place the metal in the ammonium sulphate solution for anodizing. The lower end of the spectrum will be produced.

6 Backgrounds that blend from one colour and merge into another can be created by lifting the piece out of the anodizing bath, which gradually increases the voltage in proportion to the area applied. In this way you can create the effects of sky, sunset, sea and so on.

Bending

Bending and shaping metal can bring an extra dimension to your work, allowing the light to reflect from it in unexpected and interesting ways. Curves, bends and twists can be made into attractive features, but for maximum effect they must be as smooth and as clean as possible so that the metal flows from one surface to the next.

If you are holding metal in a vice, you must cover the serrated edges on the inside of the vice with several layers of masking tape or protect the metal itself with masking tape. Many vices have additional "safe" jaws, which are made from rubber and which fit neatly over the serrated edges, and some small vices have plastic jaws.

Before you begin, decide exactly where you want the curve to be and how smooth or steep it should be. Your aim must be to get the bend right first time. Although it is possible to unbend metal, it is much more satisfactory to get it right at the first attempt. Keep your pattern or design close at hand, and after each bend lay your work on the design to check that the curve is correct. A small mistake at this stage can easily make the whole piece wrong. If you want to

make two identical curves – in a pair of earrings, for example – make the first bend in one piece, then work on the next before returning to the first. It is much easier to repeat a small step than to have to remember a series of steps.

Always try to make a clean bend rather than an overworked one. Work around a former whenever you can, and always use the correct pliers. Place the curved or rounded nose of your pliers on the inside of the curve, holding the outside with the flat edge of the pliers. If you use the wrong profile – the flat nose on the inside of a curve, for instance – you can create marks in soft metal that are difficult to remove.

Remember that most aids to bending metal are harder than the metal itself and will mark the metal if they are used incorrectly. Try to use them as precisely as possible. Among

the most under-rated tools and ones that will leave no marks are your fingers and thumbs: they may not always be the right tools but they can be useful.

It is worth keeping a supply of copper wire and sheets of different thicknesses to hand. Before bending a precious metal, work through the design in copper so that any problems can be identified and solved.

Straightening wire
It is much easier to bend wire or sheet metal that is straight or flat. Wire is usually supplied in rather loose, large coils, which do not need straightening. Unless you are bending a piece that needs to be springy – a brooch pin, for example – always work with well-annealed metal. Once metal becomes work hardened it is much more difficult to bend correctly. You can feel the

difference with your fingers between annealed and hard metal. If the wire has kinks in it or has been previously bent, work as shown here or anneal the wire, quench it in water and dry it. Then place one end in the vice and fasten it tightly. Hold the other end in a pair of serrated-edge pliers and pull the wire sharply straight towards you. You will feel the wire lengthen slightly as it straightens.

Flattening sheet metal
Place the annealed sheet between two smooth steel surfaces, both of which are larger than the sheet to be flattened. Strike the top surface

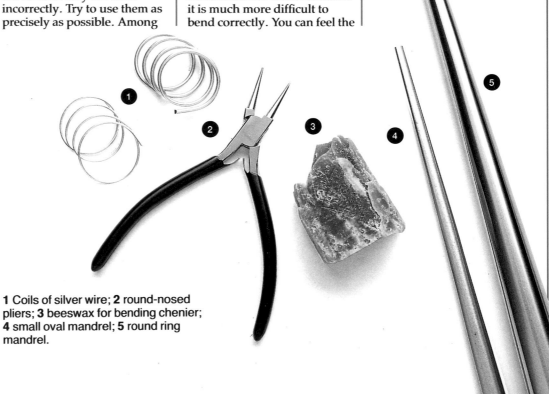

1 Coils of silver wire; **2** round-nosed pliers; **3** beeswax for bending chenier; **4** small oval mandrel; **5** round ring mandrel.

sharply with a hammer. If you are working on a very small piece, you can use the hammer alone, but you must make sure that the head of the hammer completely covers the metal; if it does not, the hammer will leave marks in the soft surface of the metal.

SEE ALSO

- Annealing 14–15
- Hammering 84–85

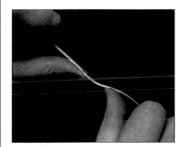

Straightening kinked wire
1 Hold the wire gently in both hands and push the bend upwards until the wire is level. Work along the wire, pushing gently upwards, until it is straight on that side. Turn over the wire and work along the other side in the same way.

2 Use the curved side of half-round pliers on the inside of the bend.

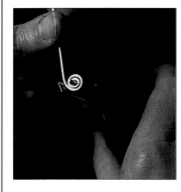

3 Use shaped pliers with one round nose and one flat nose to bend wire into a tight circle.

4 Round-nosed pliers can be used to bend wire in a different direction. Take care that you do not mark annealed metal.

Using a former
Short lengths of thick wire – more than 3mm (3⁄16in) in diameter – can be awkward to bend precisely. Take an over-length piece of wire and bend it around a former, pulling both ends together and crossing them over each other until you have achieved the correct curve. You can then cut away

the extra length from each end. This method is useful when you are bending chenier or when you are shaping a neckpiece.

To make repeating sections for a chain, saw off the heads from suitably sized nails. Place a tracing of the pattern on a block of soft wood and hammer in the nails on the inside and outside of the curves of the pattern. Leaving an extra length of wire to start and holding it firmly with a pair of pliers, use the other hand to bend the wire through the nails.

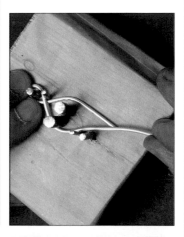

Making metal springy
To give a sprung bracelet tension, curl it around a mandrel that is smaller than the finished diameter of the bracelet and hit it with a wooden mallet or a flat-headed steel hammer,

gradually increasing the diameter while you hit it with the mallet or hammer. Continue to work the bracelet up the mandrel until it is the correct size.

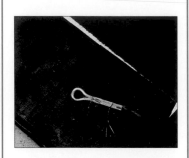

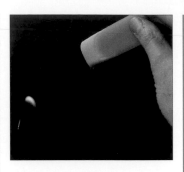

Bending section wire

1 Bend D-section wire with half-round pliers. You can file a groove into the lower end of the pliers, which will give a better purchase when you hold the wire. Use flat-nosed pliers to keep the D-section flat as it comes from the half-round pliers.

2 To make a "reef knot" ring bend a loop in D-section wire with half-round pliers.

4 Run some hard solder up the middle of two D-section wires.

Bending chenier wire

1 Before it is bent, the inside of the chenier wire must be filled so that the sides do not buckle. Warm the chenier by playing a gentle flame along the length of the wire. The heat from the flame will allow the beeswax to drip slowly into the chenier. You can also fill the chenier with fine sand, salt or warmed pitch.

5 Repeat steps 2, 3 and 4 for the other side, then slip the two ends inside the two loops and pull them together. Hold one end in a vice, grip the other end with pliers and pull tight. Cut the ends to length and solder them together with easy solder.

2 Use both hands to bend the chenier around a mandrel.

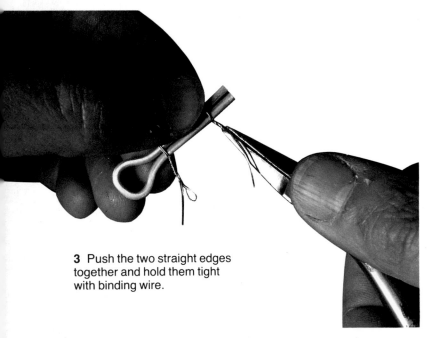

3 Push the two straight edges together and hold them tight with binding wire.

6 Use a mallet to tap the ring into shape around the mandrel.

3 Tap the wire gently around a mandrel with a mallet until it is the correct shape.

4 Place the metal in the vice so that the line you wish to bend is parallel to, and just visible above, the jaws of the vice. Tap it down cleanly with your mallet.

5 Alternatively, place the metal on a flat bed and hold the metal along the filed line in a pair of flat-nosed pliers. Push it over until the metal is bent at 90 degrees.

6 If you cannot reach the filed line with your pliers, use a steel former, held in a vice, to bend up the metal.

7 When you are bending up the sides of the base of a box, make sure that all the corner edges are filed to an angle of 45 degrees. This makes a neat join for soldering.

Bending sheets
1 Scribe along the line you wish to bend – in this case for the base of a box.

2 File along the scribed line with a three- or four-sided file until you have made a groove that is just more than half the thickness of the metal.

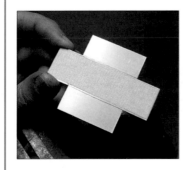

3 Protect any part of the metal that may come into contact with the jaws of the vice or use "safe" jaws.

Casting

Casting is a technique by which it is possible to create shapes that would otherwise involve an enormous amount of waste. It is also used to re-create gently flowing lines of the kind that are comparatively easy to achieve in a soft medium such as wax but that are difficult to reproduce in metal. Casting is also, of course, a means by which many identical pieces can be made, either for a mass-market or to make, for example, chains with identical links.

There are three main methods of casting. Two of these – cuttlefish casting and the lost wax method – are available to people working at home, while the third involves the production of a rubber mould, which, while possible to do in the home workshop, is expensive and requires a lot of space and special equipment and is not, therefore, viable unless it is being used almost every day. This last process is most often carried out by a commercial company working from a model you have made yourself.

Tools and materials

Several kinds of wax are available for creating the models used in casting. Among these are sheets of **flexible wax,** supplied in thicknesses from 3 to 25mm (⅛ to 1in); **blocks for carving; moulding wax,** which is worked by hand; **tubes and bars,** which can be used to make rings; and **sprue wax,** which is supplied as rods in

1 Selection of wax modelling tools;
2 cuttlefish bone;
3 moulding wax; 4 block of carving wax; 5 wax sheets in different thicknesses;
6 methylated spirit lamp for warming the modelling tools.

different sizes for attaching to models. Choose the most appropriate wax for the model you want to create.

You will also need one or two little carving tools and a craft knife. Keep a small flame burning – the pilot light of a soldering torch or a little methylated spirit lamp with a small wick, for example – so that you can keep warming the carving tool when you need to join pieces of wax together and to smooth over the surface of the wax. An electric "pen" worker can be used to join different grades of wax and is useful for shaping and moulding.

Cuttlefish casting

This is a very quick and simple method and can be done in one of two ways. The first, as shown in steps that follow, is simply to carve the required shape and depth of pattern into one side of the halved cuttlefish bone.

Cuttlefish casting

1 Use the thickest part of the bone for casting. Cut away the top and bottom ends so that it is almost square.

2 Cut down through the centre of the bone. Do not exert much pressure because the bone will cut very easily and aim to make the cut in a single pass of the saw so that the two pieces fit together perfectly. If necessary, lay the two halves on some wet and dry papers, used dry, and work in gentle circular movements until the inner surfaces are completely flat and smooth.

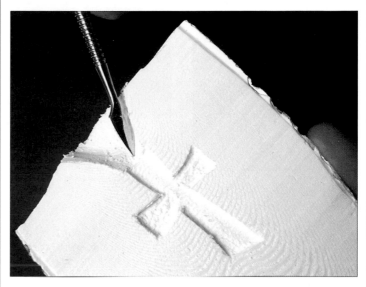

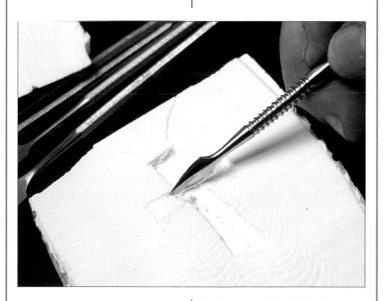

3 Use a modelling tool to carve your design directly into the bone. You will find it a very dense but soft material that carves easily.

4 In the top of the bone, cut out a rounded channel. This channel, which must be slightly deeper than the design, is the duct through which the molten metal will be poured. Make it fairly large.

5 Place the two sections of the bone together, making sure the fit is perfect, and fasten securely with binding wire. Prop up the bone next to the soldering block. Cut up some scrap silver into little pieces and place them in a small crucible with some flux powder. It is difficult to estimate how much metal specific projects will require, but prepare more than you think will be necessary.

6 Heat the silver in the crucible. Pick up the crucible with a pair of long-handle tongs just when the silver begins to run up into a molten ball.

7 Keep the flame on the silver as you bring the crucible to the channel in the cuttlefish bone. Pour the silver into the bone.

9 Neaten the edges of the casting and burnish to highlight the high edges.

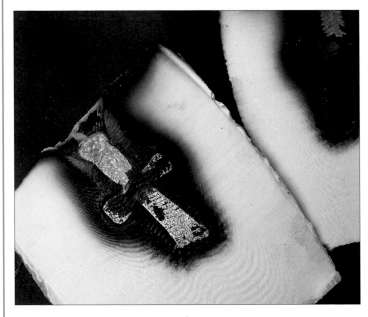

8 When it is cool, cut the binding wire and open the bone. The cuttlefish bone will have turned black around the area of casting and cannot be used again. Make sure the silver is quite cold before you touch it. You can run it under cold water to speed the cooling down process.

The alternative method consists of using a cuttlefish bone to make a model – in perspex or metal, for example – or to use a found object of a suitable shape. The bone is prepared as described in steps 1 and 2, but the object is then pushed into half the bone until it is buried to about half its depth. The model should be positioned so that its heaviest part is towards the bottom of the bone.

Lost wax casting
This technique involves making a wax model that is supported on a conical stand mounted on a rubber or ceramic base. The model is surrounded by a metal sleeve or flask, which fits tightly onto the base, and a plaster/silica mix, known as investment, is poured into the flask and allowed to set. The flask is then placed in a heated kiln to burn away the wax, which leaves an empty mould within the investment. The wax melts and burns away, and the impression of the mould is left in the hardened investment. When all the wax has burnt away and the investment is the correct temperature, the flask is removed from the kiln and placed into a "centrifugal" casting machine which is held in tension by a spring. The metal is then melted in the crucible which is secured in place against the open end of the flask, and when it is completely molten, the heat is removed, the spring latch of the casting machine released and the molten metal flung into the mould.

When the wax model has been completed and sprued, it is weighed, and weight of the wax is multiplied by 11 for silver, by 18 for 22 carat gold, by 14 for 14 carat gold and by 12 for 9 carat gold to find the weight of the metal needed for casting.

Preparing the investment

Mix the investment in water that is at room temperature in the proportions of 4 parts water to 10 parts investment. Once the investment has been added to the water it must be mixed and poured as quickly as possible because it begins to harden after about 10 minutes. If the wax model is exceptionally detailed apply a coat of investment before you begin pouring; this will help to prevent air bubbles being trapped on the surface of the model, which is to be avoided at all costs because they would be cast as silver blobs.

When pouring the investment into the flask, it is important to bring as many air bubbles as possible to the surface. Hold the flask in both hands and gently bang it on your working surface a few times.

The rubber or ceramic base is then removed from the flask and the flask placed into the kiln. It should be placed with the sprue opening facing the floor of the kiln and it should be supported, either on ceramic legs or between two ceramic kiln bases, so that the wax can melt and drop out of the investment. The kiln is set to approx 150°C and this temperature should be held for approx 1 hour to allow all the wax to burn out and then increased to approx 370°C for another hour. The temperature is then increased further – up to approx 700°C for the last two hours of the burn out.

Use long-handled tongs to remove the flask from the kiln and place it in the centrifugal machine. Place the weighed and cut up metal in the crucible with some flux powder, and use a strong torch to melt it. Do not include any solder in the metal used for casting and when you are cutting up scrap, put any soldered joints back into your scrap box.

The machine is sprung into position and released, and the centrifugal force created shoots the molten metal out of the mouth of the crucible into the spruc channel of the flask. Pick up the flask with the long-handle tongs and place it in a bucket of water. The investment will break away to reveal the metal casting. Remove the sprue and file and finish the piece.

Lost wax casting

1 Mark out the design on the modelling wax. The design can be accurately drawn with dividers, a scribe or something similar and then the details of the motifs can be cut away with modelling tools. Bear in mind that the pattern can be cut and modelled very finely, and that the finished piece in silver will weight about 11 times more than the wax model.

2 When the modelling is finished, cut away the pattern from the block of wax and file away any marks made by the blade of the saw. Make any final refinements and smoothing to the wax.

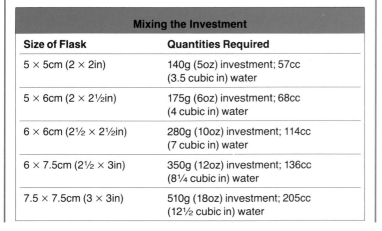

3 If you wish, gently play a flame over the model to soften the edges. Attach a sprue by heating up the modelling tool in the flame and placing it smoothly between the model and the sprue. Hold them in place until the wax has set.

Mixing the Investment	
Size of Flask	**Quantities Required**
5 × 5cm (2 × 2in)	140g (5oz) investment; 57cc (3.5 cubic in) water
5 × 6cm (2 × 2½in)	175g (6oz) investment; 68cc (4 cubic in) water
6 × 6cm (2½ × 2½in)	280g (10oz) investment; 114cc (7 cubic in) water
6 × 7.5cm (2½ × 3in)	350g (12oz) investment; 136cc (8¼ cubic in) water
7.5 × 7.5cm (3 × 3in)	510g (18oz) investment; 205cc (12½ cubic in) water

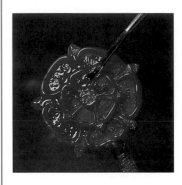

4 Melt the sprue onto the top of the base of the flask and paint the model with a wetting agent.

6 Tie a polythene bag, opened at the bottom, around the flask to prevent spills then pour the investment into the flask so that it is just over the top of the flask. Vibrate the whole thing to remove air bubbles.

8 Give the flask and base a sharp knock to separate the two sections. If you are using a flask with a rubber base, simply peel it away. The wax sprue at the top of the channel should be visible.

9 Leave the investment to dry thoroughly for 2–4 hours, then place it in a kiln so that the sprue is towards the floor of the kiln. Set the kiln to about 150°C (300°F) and leave it at that temperature for about 1 hour. Increase the temperature to about 700°C (1290°F) for a further 2 hours. Then reduce the temperature of the kiln to about 500°C (930°F) for the last hour so that the investment is a suitable temperature when it receives the molten metal.

5 Place the flask onto the base and make sure there is space of at least 1cm (½in) between the model and the sides of the flask. The model should be 2–3m (about 1in) below the level of the top rim of the flask.

7 Leave the investment to dry a little before removing the polythene bag and slicing away any excess investment at the top of the flask. Then leave to dry thoroughly 2–4 hours.

10 While the flask is in the kiln at the lower temperature, prepare the appropriate amount of silver for the casting and place it in the crucible with some flux powder. Remove the flask from the kiln, holding it in long-handled tongs, and place it in the casting machine so that the mouth of the crucible is in a direct line with the sprue channel in the flask.

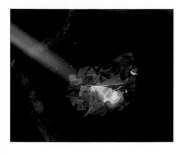

11 Melt the silver with a strong flame. You must work quickly so that the temperature of the flask does not drop too much. When the silver is molten, remove the flame and release the spring mechanism of the machine. Move away from the machine because molten silver may fly out at this point if the flask is not properly aligned or if there is some other fault with the machine or setting-up process. Allow the machine to stop completely before you remove the flask.

12 Using tongs to hold the flask, place it in a bucket of cool water. The investment will fall apart and reveal the casting. Clean away all the remaining investment with pumice paste and a toothbrush and use a small steel tool to remove any investment that has stuck in the nooks and crannies of the design.

Commercial casting
This is the process by which a rubber mould can be used many times to create large quantities of articles. In essence, a rubber mould is made around a silver or rhodium-plated model which has a sprue attached. The rubber mould is cut in half to release the model in such a way that it can be exactly relocated. Warm wax is injected into the realigned mould and removed so that more wax can be introduced to produce yet another model. All the wax models are mounted on a "tree", which is placed in an investment and cast in the same way as the lost wax method but on a much larger scale.

To make a good casting, You must make a really well-finished model, which is sent away to be cast commercially. If you are in any doubt about the positioning of the sprue, ask for advice from the company or leave it to the company to attach the sprue.

2 Polish the model to give it a very smooth finish. Any scratches or file marks left at this stage will have to be removed on every piece subsequently made.

3 The commercial company makes a rubber mould around your model. This mould is then held together and injected with wax so that as many wax models as necessary can be made from just the one mould.

13 Pierce away the sprue and file the edges to make the piece ready for finishing.

Preparing a model for commercial casting
1 Make the model in nickel silver or silver and attach a sprue with easy solder. Make sure that the area around the join has enough solder to allow a smooth flow.

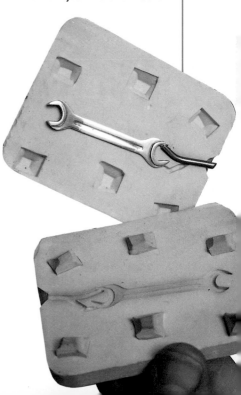

Catches and Joints

As you work through the steps illustrated here most of the techniques will become self-evident. However, there are some points to bear in mind when you make catches and joints for pieces of jewellery.

Catches
Several types of catch are available ready-made, so when you are designing a piece you should consider whether a hand-made catch will help to create the effect you want to achieve better than a bought one. For example, you might want to consider the time you will have to spend in fashioning a tiny box catch for a small chain when a ready-made one will look just as good.

Standard silver, which is a comparatively soft metal, is not always suitable for use on a spring-type catch. Silver can, of course, be made hard and springy by hitting it with a hammer on a steel support, but even this will not necessarily make it strong enough for your purposes. Nickel silver and steel could be used to make the spring, but they should not be soldered to precious metal if you want the work to be hallmarked. These metals could be riveted on or held in place under tension.

Remember that catches are fitted when all other work has been finished, and usually soft or easy solder is used to attach them. Some bought catches – the bolt rings, for example, which are widely used to close chains – have a little steel spring within them. It is better to buy a catch to which the attachment ring has already been soldered so that any additional soldering will be done on the adjoining jump ring. Try to keep the heat of your torch away from the bolt ring as much as you can when you are soldering, perhaps by placing a small sheet of mica over the ring while you work.

Do not quench after soldering because if the bolt ring is immersed in acid it may be difficult to remove all traces of acid and the steel may contaminate the metal around it. Also, if it is quenched while hot, the steel will be softened.

Spring T-bars on cuff link fittings should be removed before the back fittings are soldered to the front, because they contain a piece of steel that acts as a spring within the bar. They should be replaced and riveted in place when all other work is complete.

SEE ALSO

- Riveting 108–111
- Bending 18–21
- Soldering 112–115

1 Gold padlock catch; **2** silver bolt rings of different sizes; **3** silver swivel catch; **4** jointing tool for holding chenier and wire while cutting a straight edge; **5** pair of dividers; **6** round-nosed pliers.

Making a figure-of-eight catch

1 Use tweezers to hold the end of a piece of wire against the side of a charcoal block. Concentrate the flame just above the end until the metal begins to run into a ball. Withdraw the flame when the ball is the size you want.

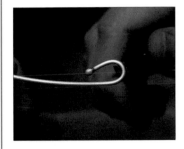

2 Use half-round pliers to make the first curve.

3 Cut the other end to length and form another ball as in step 1. Shape the figure-of-eight and solder one end to close the loop.

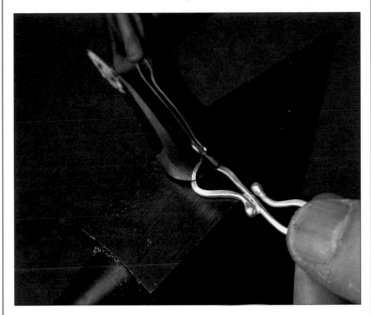

4 Place each loop in turn on the anvil and tap it lightly to flatten it and harden it.

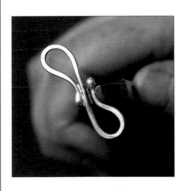

5 Open out the free loop slightly to make it easier to slip it into the ring on the necklace. Place a jump ring through the soldered loop and attach it to one end of the necklace.

Soldered catch

1 Solder a length of wire to a small section of wire that is approximately twice the diameter of the first. Cut the wire to length.

2 Solder the smaller end of the wire to the last section of the necklace.

3 Take the last section of the other end of the necklace and pierce a hole in the centre that is large enough to push the larger end of the wire through. Cut a channel to within 3–5mm (less than ¼in) of the end of the section. The channel should be just wide enough to accommodate the thinner wire.

4 Place the head through the hole and pull the two ends away from each other.

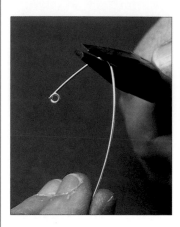

Simple catch

1 Curl a small loop in one end of a length of wire. Leave about 2cm (¾in) before bending a right angle.

2 Bend a second right angle in the wire. This defines the width of the catch. Make another small loop in the other end of the wire and cut away the excess wire.

3 Use half-round pliers to make a slight outward curve on the top end of the loop. Place the two sides around a former, such as the short end of a drill bit held in a vice, and pull the side together.

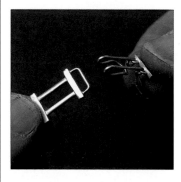

4 Attach the two loops of the catch to the last section of a chain and solder on a wire loop, which should be just wider than the catch, to the other end of the chain.

Making catches for fabric

The catches shown in this and the next sequence can be used with fabric. The ones shown here are used to fasten a necklace made from braided silk.

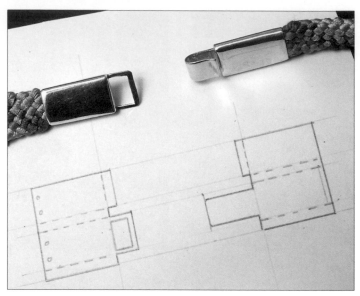

1 The two halves of this silver catch are made from a single sheet of silver. Calculate the left-hand pattern by doubling the width of the braid and adding to that measurement twice the depth of the braid. The loop for the catch goes on one of the longer sides and the tab, equal to the depth, goes on the other long side. Draw dotted lines to indicate where the metal will be bent. Draw the right-hand pattern in the same way, but instead of a loop on one side allow sufficient metal to fold back on itself to make a catch. This section must be narrower than the loop so that it will fit into it.

2 Cut the pattern from the metal and use a four-sided file to make grooves along the dotted lines. Bend up the pattern and solder them down the inside edges. Clean and polish before fitting it to the braid. Either fix two rivets through the layers of silver and braid or make two silver screws using the tap and die set. The ends of the screws will need to be filed flush with the metal.

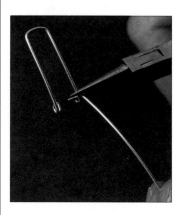

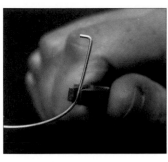

Making an interlocking catch

1 Bend a loop with one straight end and a U-shaped curve at the other. Solder together the ends at the straight end.

2 Use round-nosed pliers to make a "waist" in the loop.

3 Harden the loop by hammering it on an anvil. Make a second loop in the same way.

4 Slip one end of the necklace through the straight end section of the loop; repeat at the other end. Check the length before sewing the fabric to itself to hold the loops in place.

5 The catch holds one loop being turned sideways so that it slips through the other loop. Use half-round pliers to bend the end of one loop up and the end of the other loop down so that they sit comfortably together.

Catches for chains

1 Make a small wire loop and thread about 2.5cm (1in) of chain onto it. Place the loop in the middle of a wire bar that has a diameter of about 1.5mm (1/16in). Flux the join carefully so that no flux gets onto the chain. Place a paillon of easy solder to the join and solder the loop to the bar. Paint a little rouge on the chain to protect it against the solder.

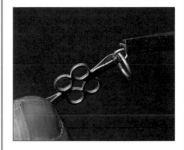

2 Solder up a ring that is large enough for the bar to pass through it. Use a smaller jump ring, which can be soldered with easy solder, to attach this to one end of the necklace.

3 Join the short length of chain to the other end of the main chain using a jump ring, which should be isolated and soldered with easy solder. The bar is threaded through the large ring to hold the necklace together.

Making a spring catch

1 To make a catch about 2cm (3/4in) long, take a length of D-section wire about 3cm (1 1/4in) long. Drill a hole in one end and file the end to make it round. Halfway along the flat side of the wire, file a groove that is just more than half the depth of the wire.

2 Carefully bend the D-section wire back on itself, flat sides together, at the groove. File another little groove all around the ends, about 5mm (1/4in) from the end.

3 Bend what will be the top end of the catch up by 90 degrees.

4 Place the folded end of the catch on the anvil and tap it gently with a hammer, turning it round as you hit it so that it keeps its shape. Check that the catch will fit into a piece of chenier, which should have an inside diameter that is slightly larger than the width of the flat side of the D-section wire. If the catch will not fit, file carefully all around until it does.

5 Cut a piece of chenier approximately 2cm (¾in) long. Solder a ring to one end. The inside diameter of the ring should be slightly smaller than the inside of the chenier.

6 Solder a flat piece of silver to the other end of the chenier. Trim it with a piercing saw and neaten the edge with a file. Solder a ring or loop to this flat end. The chain will be attached to this loop.

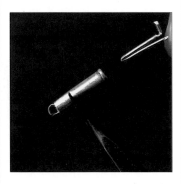

7 Fit the spring end into the chenier catch. If it does not click home you will have to make sure that the groove filed at the point where the end turns up is deep enough to fit under the wire ring soldered around the chenier. File two or three small grooves in the top of the tab to make it easier to push down.

Hinges

Hinges are used whenever full movement in a single plane is required. The hinge described here would be appropriate for a small box. On a small object the hinge needs to be made of only three sections, and the wire used for the pin should fit closely through the chenier.

If the hinge needs to be set slightly away from the piece – as may be the case on a large, round locket or a pocket watch, for example – the sections of the chenier for the hinge must be held in a bracket made to fit the side of the circle. You will need two sizes of chenier for this – the size required for the hinge itself and a larger size into which the smaller piece will fit. Determine the length of the hinge. Cut off a section to the requisite length from the larger chenier and then cut it through the centre lengthways to make two long, semicircular sections.

Hard solder a strip of silver, about 1cm (½in) wide, along the length of one semicircular section of chenier so that it is flush with the top edge. Do the same with the other semicircular section. File or cut away the top quarter on the side length of the chenier not soldered to the silver strip. Repeat on the other piece. The chenier for the hinge is placed in the semicircular curved part of the bracket (similar to the method shown).

An alternative way of placing chenier in the hinge is to divide the length required into three or five equal sections and to cut three or five lengths of chenier to fit. File a little edge back from both ends of each section to allow freer movement, then line up the sections of chenier, side by side, in one half of the semicircular strips you have just made. Dab a tiny amount of flux between the first, third and fifth sections and the semicircle they are sitting in and place a paillon of solder in the same place. Place the other half of the bracket on top, dab a little flux between the second and fourth section and position a paillon of solder. Heat the whole hinge until the solder just tacks the pieces together, but take care that one piece of solder does not run onto the adjoining piece of chenier. Quench, pickle and rinse the two halves before soldering the chenier to each side more thoroughly.

To fit the bracket to the locket or watch, place the flat strip section of the bracket under the circular locket or watch at the point of attachment and use a scribe to mark around the curved edge. Pierce away the scribed line and file it smooth so that the bracket can be neatly soldered to the top section of the locket or watch. Scribe a similar line on the other bracket and pierce it out as before so that it can be neatly soldered to the bottom half of the locket or watch. The hinge can then be assembled with a rivet.

Making a hinge
1 File a groove in the sides of the pieces that are to be hinged. Use either a parallel round file or the side of a joint round-edge file. The groove must be deep enough to allow the chenier that is used as the hinge to sit snugly inside.

2 Place a length of chenier against the groove and use dividers to mark the exact length of the groove.

3 Divide and mark the length of chenier into five equal sections. Use a piercing saw to cut halfway through the chenier at these four points.

4 File away the second and fourth sections to just over halfway through the chenier. Cut the fifth section from the chenier length.

5 Place the shaped chenier in the groove in the side of one piece of metal, with the filed away areas facing into the groove. Place a small amount of flux and a paillon of solder at the points where the first, third and fifth sections fit into the groove and solder them in place.

6 Remove the remainder of the second and fourth sections with your piercing saw.

7 Use dividers to measure the gaps left and mark these points on a piece of chenier. Cut off two pieces and file them until they fit perfectly into the gaps left by the second and fourth sections. Check again that they fit.

8 Place the two pieces of metal side by side and use dividers to mark on the second piece the points at which the gaps occur. These measurements must be very precisely measured and marked. Place the two pieces of chenier between these marks.

9 Solder the two pieces of chenier into the groove on the metal.

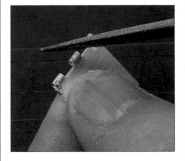

10 Carefully file around the edges of all the chenier pieces to allow them to move freely against each other.

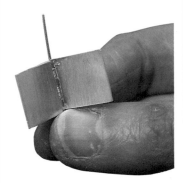

11 Thread a length of wire through all the chenier sections. Cut it to length and rivet over the ends.

Universal joints

Universal joints are used when full movement in two planes is required. A simple jump ring is a kind of universal joint, but, as we have seen, it is not always appropriate for a well-designed piece. A universal joint can be hidden within a tube or it can be made into a separate entity.

The joint is made by attaching a piece of wire to one side of the chain, pivoting it on another piece, which is attached to the other side of the chain. The design must always take into account the fact that the wire must be strong enough to have a hole drilled through it to take the smaller wire. Both wires have to pass through a central pin, which can be shaped to match your design.

The principle of the universal joint can be applied by placing the joints of a chain or necklace on different planes. For example, a chain could be made extremely flexible if small rectangular sections were twisted through 90 degrees in the centre and hinges soldered to each end.

Making a universal joint

1 Drill through the tabs at one end of a chenier section a hole through which a wire approximately 1.2mm (¹⁄₃₂in) in diameter will pass. (For making chenier, see page 40.)

2 The second wire for the joint must be small enough to pass through the first wire – wire about 0.5mm in diameter should be suitable. Copper wire has been used here for clarity. Drill a hole for this finer wire through the tabs at the other end of the chenier section.

3 Take a piece of chenier that will fit inside the chenier used for the chain and drill a hole through it that is the same size as the hole for the fine wire, positioning the hole about 3mm (¹⁄₈in) from the edge. Cut off the chenier so that it is about 6mm (¹⁄₄in) long and round off the edges with a file.

4 Offer up the smaller chenier to the chenier used for the chain to make certain that it will move freely inside it.

5 Take the thicker wire and thread it through the tabs in the chenier and through the centre of the small piece of chenier so that the small piece is held between the tabs. Hold the wire steady while you drill through it a hole that will take the 0.5mm wire. Locate the drill by placing it through the hole made in step 3.

6 Place the section of chain over the next section so that the small holes line up.

7 Thread the finer wire through the tabs in the chenier, through the smaller hole of the piece within and through the wire within that piece. Cut the wires to length and rivet the fine wire in place. This holds the larger one, which does not need riveting as well. The smaller holes in the chenier will need to be countersunk for the rivet.

Making a box catch

Box catches are used when a secure fitting is needed on a fairly heavy article of jewellery such as a necklace or a bracelet. Make the width of the box suit the overall dimensions of the piece with which it is used.

1 Mark four lines on a piece of silver to show the width and the height. File grooves along each of these lines and cut the silver to length. File the sides that meet when the box is folded to 45 degrees.

2 Fold the silver along the grooves to form a box and solder together (see Bending, pages 18–21). At the same time, apply flux along all the inside corners of the box and run some hard solder along these points. This strengthens the area you have filed to facilitate bending.

3 Solder a plate of silver to one end of the box. Pickle, rinse and dry and then pierce away the excess metal.

6 Place a small piece of silver across the area you have just removed and solder it in place. Trim away excess with a piercing saw.

9 Make the snap fastener from a piece of silver that will, when folded over, fit into the box. The silver should be slightly less than the internal width of the box and about twice as long, although it is not crucial if the catch does not reach to the end of the box. You also need a strip at one end that is the same thickness as the metal used to make the slotted front of the box. Mark the appropriate lines on the silver and file a groove at the halfway point. Do not file the line indicating the thickness of the metal. Carefully bend over the silver along the filed line.

11 Cut out a small square of silver and file two or three grooves in the top edge. This tab should fit into the slot filed in the box section and it should be about 25 per cent longer than the length of the groove.

4 At the open end of the box mark a line that is the same thickness as the metal used for the plate at the other end.

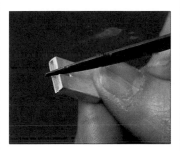

7 Mark the centre of the box on the side you have just soldered and file a groove through the soldered strip and about a quarter of the way into the box.

12 Use easy solder to attach the tab to the top part of the snap section, leaving the last quarter of its length overhanging the edge.
Tap the snap end down on an anvil to make it springy. If you alter the shape while you are doing this, file it to size so that it will fit the box.

5 Use a piecing saw to cut into the box along the marked line, halfway down the sides of the box. Cut away this fillet and file the edges smooth.

8 Use easy solder to fit a ring to the solid end of the box. Clean the box and finish it with wet and dry papers.

10 Solder a piece of silver at 90° to the longer section of the snap fastener and solder an attachment ring to the back of it.

13 Fit the two sections together. You should be able to hear a click as the snap locates behind the front of the box. Mark on the back plate of the snap where it needs filing. Neaten up all edges. Clean and polish.

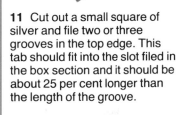

Chain Making

With so many variations in the kinds of materials, linking systems, colours, lengths, weights and fastenings, chain making can be an opportunity to let your imagination have free rein. There is also great satisfaction in making an object that is complete in itself.

The decorative aspects of chains follow from their functional aspects. If two sections of a chain are linked together with a single wire ring, the piece will be flexible because the sections will be able to move around the ring to form a curve as well as being able to move back and forth to curve in the opposite direction. A simple jump ring, although ideally suited to this purpose, does not always suit the design and may look ill-considered or simply boring. Therefore, while aiming to accommodate the principle of the jump ring, the challenge of chain making lies in the ways in which the simple jump ring's function can be translated into a decorative form.

Planning the chain

Before you make a chain, there are several points to consider. First, you must determine the length. If it is to be an exact length, you will need to work out the number and size of each section. This may not be critical on a long chain, but if you are making a shorter one (about 40cm (16in) long), you should draw a circle with this circumference and divide it up until you have the correct number and length of sections.

Remember that the fastening is important, too. If it is made to be an integral part of the design it will bring the whole thing together. Although bolt rings are useful, they can look rather like after-thoughts and spoil the effect of a well-designed necklace or chain.

You must also take the weight of the chain into consideration, and think about the weight of each link in terms of the sections it will be joining. A heavy chain will need a sturdy link; a light chain will need a proportionately delicate link.

Soldering chains

It is not always necessary to solder the links of a chain, but if they are not soldered the links should be sufficiently strong that they cannot be pulled apart by hand. For information on soldering chains, see pages 112–115.

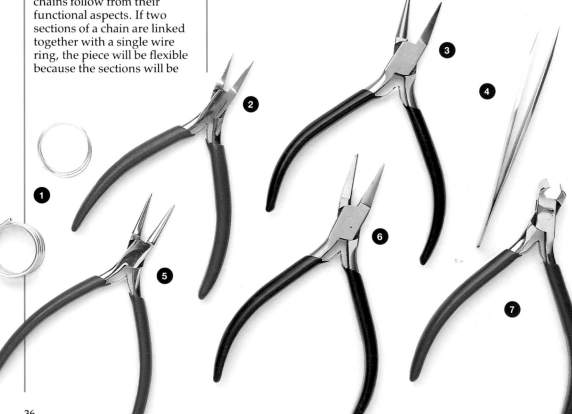

SEE ALSO

- Bending 18–21
- Drilling 50–51
- Polishing 104–105
- Soldering 112–115
- Using wire 128–133

1 Coils of silver; 2 flat-nosed pliers; 3 round flat pliers; 4 stainless steel tweezers; 5 round-nosed pliers; 6 half-round pliers; 7 oblique cutters.

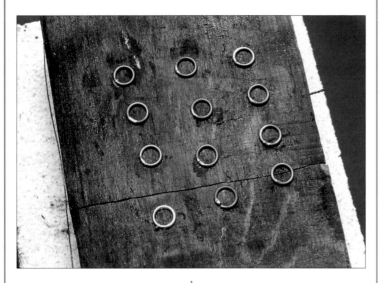

4 Open the rings by holding them in two pairs of flat-nosed pliers and twisting one pair of pliers away from you and the other pair towards you.

Simple linked chain
1 Solder the joins in a sufficient number of 6mm (⅓in) jump rings to make the length of chain you require. Quench, rinse and dry.

5 Link the rings so that they lie in the same direction. Flux the join and resolder it. You may not need to add more solder, but try one ring first to check. When you are resoldering, work on one link at a time and make sure that the join is not resting on the next link, holding the ring upright in a pair of insulated tweezers.

2 Hammer the rings flat on an anvil or flat plate, then file away all excess solder.

3 Pierce through the solder join of each ring.

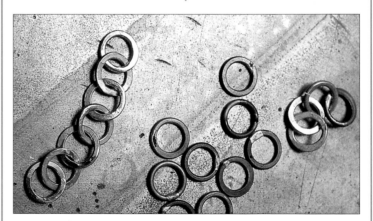

6 This method makes an attractive hammered chain, which can be thoroughly pickled and cleaned when it is finished (see Polishing, pages 104–105).

An oval link chain

1 Oval links can be made by soldering up round links, which are then stretched over the opened nose of a pair of round-nosed pliers.

A double-loop chain
1 Solder up lots of 0.5mm rings.

2 Stretch the rings into ovals then fasten an old drill bit securely in a vice and use the straight end as a former around which the loops can be bent.

3 Bring the two ends of each loop together, loop one link into the next, and continue to make a chain, closing up each link as you work.

2 Half the links can be twisted through 360 degrees, while the remaining links are cut open at the solder join in the long side and the twisted links slipped in. The joins are then resoldered.

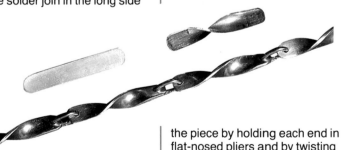

Simple twisted chain

Make a simple twisted chain by cutting sheet metal into pieces about 25 x 5mm (1 x ¼in), filing the ends to round them and drilling a hole in each end. Twist the piece by holding each end in flat-nosed pliers and by twisting one pair away from you by 90 degrees and the other pair towards you by 90 degrees. Join the lengths together with jump rings, soldering each ring at the join.

4 This makes a flexible, lightweight chain.

3 Drill a hole in the centre of each end tab.

4 Use a file to make the square ends round.

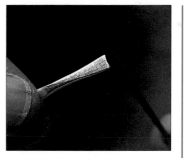

Using wire and chenier
1 Cut equal lengths of round wire, approximately 2mm (¹⁄₁₆in) in diameter. Spread the ends of the wire by hammering them out on a flat metal plate. Use a half-round file to shape the end into a gentle curve.

Linking square wire
1 Use your dividers to measure and mark a length of 3 x 3mm (about ³⁄₁₆ x ³⁄₁₆in) silver wire into equal pieces, each about 3cm (1¼in) long. Cut out.

2 Bend some fine chenier so that it follows the same curve and cut it into pieces that will fit into the centre of each curve. Use hard solder to solder a chenier piece to each end of each section.

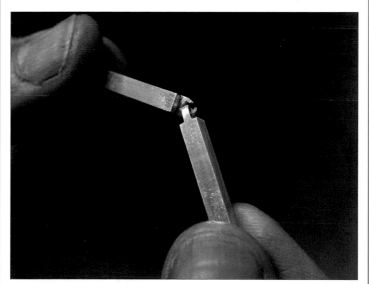

2 Mentally number the sides of each length from 1 to 4 and cut into sides 1 and 3 for 3mm (about ³⁄₁₆in) at one end. Cut away the outside edges. Repeat this step at the other end, but on sides 2 and 4.

5 Pierce through one end loop and open it just wide enough to slip through the opposite end loop of the next section. Carefully solder the join. Continue like this with each section until you have the right length chain.

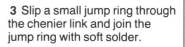

3 Slip a small jump ring through the chenier link and join the jump ring with soft solder.

Linking chenier

1 Bend chenier to the correct curve for a short necklace (see Bending, pages 18–21) and cut it into sections. Use dividers to mark the four quarters of the diameter at each end of every piece.

2 Drill a hole through two opposite end sections of the chenier.

3 Place the chenier in a chenier holder and pierce out the top and bottom quarters.

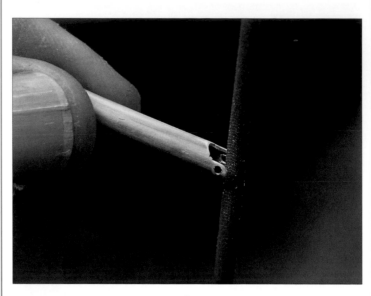

4 At the other end, drill a hole through two opposite end sections of the chenier, making sure that they are at the opposite side from the holes at the top end. Pierce out the two

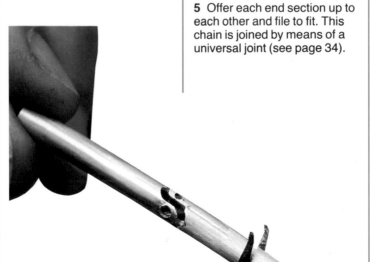

remaining side quarters. File the protruding ends to a curve and use a round needle file to neaten the inside area.

5 Offer each end section up to each other and file to fit. This chain is joined by means of a universal joint (see page 34).

Loop-in-loop chain

1 Use wire, approximately 0.65mm gauge, to make rings with a diameter of 14mm (⅝in). Lay them on a charcoal block and solder them one at a time.

2 Form each ring into an oval by stretching it over the ends of a pair of round-nosed pliers. Place three loops together into a star-shape and solder them together.

3 Solder a sprue of nickel silver or brass firmly in the centre of the three loops. Each loop must make firm contact with the sprue stick.

4 Hold the sprue in a vice and, with the ends of your fingers, gently curve each loop up.

5 Thread a single oval loop through the lowest fixed loop in the group.

6 Place a second loop through the next loop of the group, and then thread a third loop through the third loop in the sprued group.

7 Bend up the first layer of loops then the second layer of loops before inserting, in the same order as before, three more loops.

8 The third group of loops is threaded through both the first and second sets of loops.

9 Push the inner loops upwards so that they are close together.

10 Use a smooth hook – a curved burnisher, for example – to ease the hoops so that additional sets of loops can be inserted. Carry on inserting three new loops through the two previous sets of loops, curving them with your fingers as you work.

11 When the chain is 3–4cm (1¼–1½in) long, remove it from the vice and use a wooden mallet to shape it gently while it is rolled along a flat plate. Keep working in this manner until the chain is as long as you want it. When you have finished all the construction, it will need to be pulled through a large draw plate to straighten it. Place it in the vice, push the sprue end through the hole you have drilled to size and pull the chain through.

Chasing and Repoussé

Chasing is the art of controlling a small steel tool to push the lines of a pattern along the surface of the metal. The metal itself is not removed, as it would be if an engraving tool were used. Rather, it is moved sideways and compressed downwards on the surface of the metal as the tool is pushed along the line. Chasing is used to outline and define areas of metal that have been repousséd, and it is worked from the top, or visible, side of the metal. Repoussé is the art of working with punches from the back of an article to form shapes and lines that give your work a three-dimensional appearance when it is viewed from the front.

Type of punches

You will need several different punches for chasing. A **tracer punch** is used to outline the design. It has a rounded, chisel-type head, which can be rectangular, slightly curved, V-shaped, half-round and so on. The head is slightly rounded so that the metal is not cut by a sharp edge as the punch is hammered along.

A **modelling punch** has a flat, rounded head, and it is used to define areas of repousséd work by pushing down the metal around and between the raised areas. Keep the head rounded and shiny so that the metal is not marked when it is being worked.

A **matting punch** has a patterned head and is usually used to punch texture into background areas. Matting punches also vary in shape and size, and the faces of the heads can be criss-cross, striped, lined or dotted, but, like the other punches, the heads should have rounded edges. The patterned faces are not polished, because this would lead to loss of definition.

A **planishing punch** has a polished, flat face. These punches, which are made in a range of sizes, are used for smoothing over repoussé marks left by the punches used to work the back of the metal.

Circles in relief are made by a **hollow-faced punch**, which can be used on either the front or the back of the metal. The heads of these punches vary in diameter, and, as with matting punches, they are not polished so that definition is not lost. The edges are slightly rounded so that the metal is not cut by the punch.

Most repoussé work is done with an **embossing punch**, which is used to push up areas of metal from behind to create the relief on the front. These punches are usually oval, round, square or rectangular, and they have rounded edges and polished faces.

Using punches

When you use a tracer punch to make a line, the top of the punch is held at a slight angle away from you, while the bottom or face is towards you so that the line being traced is clearly visible. Hold the punch between your thumb and three

1 Pitch bowl on support. An old heavy saucepan could also be used. It is filled almost to the top with a ready-made pitch mixture; **2** selection of repoussé and matting punches.

fingers, while your little finger rests on the metal to steady and support your hand. Hit the top of the punch rhythmically with a chasing hammer – a small hammer with a broad head and a well-balanced handle – which facilitates repetitive hitting. If you are using a tracer punch to outline a curve or a V-shape, hold the punch upright and give it a single hammer blow.

Modelling and planishing punches are held in the same way as the tracer punch, and they, too, are hit with the chasing hammer.

Matting and hollow-faced punches are held upright and struck with a single hammer blow. The punch is then lifted and repositioned on the metal so that it slightly overlaps the previously punched area.

Embossing punches are held slightly away from you and hit continuously. The punch is moved across the metal and not lifted from the surface in order to form a smooth, indentation in the metal.

Holding your work

Work that is going to be chased and repousséd has to be held in a firm but "giving" medium called pitch, which is a mixture of pitch, tallow or linseed oil and plaster of Paris or pumice powder. You can add tallow or linseed oil to pitch to soften it if it becomes brittle, which sometimes happens in cold weather.

Metal will be held more firmly in the pitch if the corners of a piece are turned down. Allow a good margin around the design so that you can turn down the corners with pliers.

You will have to take the metal from the pitch several times during the chasing and repoussé process. Not only will it need annealing from time to time to keep the metal pliable, but you will have to turn it over when you have to work on the back or the front. When you remove the work, gently heat the pitch around the metal and lift up one corner with an old pair of insulated tweezers. The metal will be covered in pitch, and you have to remove this before you can continue with your work. Hold the work in the flame of your torch so that the pitch burns off. Allow the pitch to burn until it is dry and forms flakes, which will either fall off or can be blown off. Do not quench the metal until the pitch has burnt off. This method also anneals the metal.

When you put the piece back in the pitch, the indentations on the back need to be filled with pitch to provide support. The piece would collapse if a matting, tracing or planishing punch were used on unsupported metal. Keep a small, separate container of pitch and heat it up so that you can pour it into the indentations. Allow it to cool before turning the piece over and replacing it in the pitch.

SEE ALSO

- Annealing 14–15
- Hammering 84–85

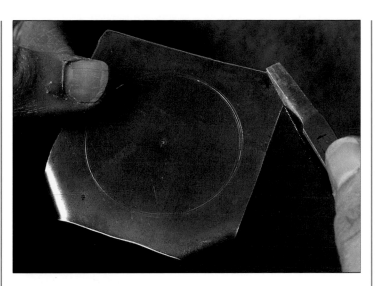

Working the metal
1 Mark on the metal the area needed for the pattern, making sure that you leave an outside border of 1–2cm (½–¾in), then bend down the corners of the metal with a pair of flat-nosed pliers.

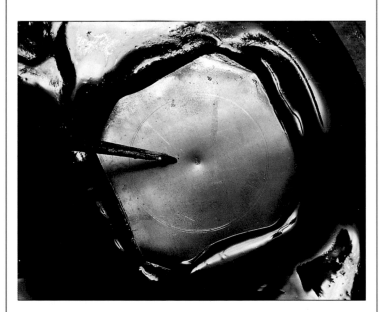

2 Heat the pitch until running and shiny, then place the metal in it. The turned-down corners, or tabs, will help to hold the metal firmly. Wet the ends of your fingers and push the pitch over the edge of the metal.

3 When the pitch is cool, rub the surface of the metal with plasticine or putty and trace the pattern through the tracing paper to the surface of your work.

5 Tap the head of the tool with gentle, rhythmic strokes with a chasing hammer while following the line.

4 Carefully remove the tracing paper and take a small chasing tool. If you are right handed hold the tool in your left hand; if you are left handed hold it in your right hand. Rest your little finger on the metal to help support and steady your hand, and hold the tool at a slight angle away from the direction of the line to be chased.

6 Hold the repoussé punch upright and use an ordinary flat-headed hammer to hit the punch.

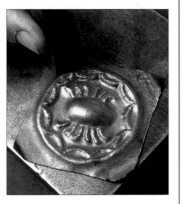

9 Pierce away the outside edges.

8 Place the work on a flat plate and gently punch down all the areas that should be flat. Work especially around the outside edge of the pattern so that it is level all round.

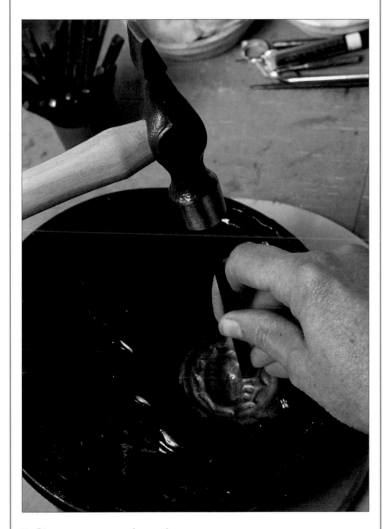

7 Choose a repoussé punch that will fit the shape you want to hammer and use the lines made by the chasing tool on the other side as a guide.

10 Use a file to tidy the edges before polishing the piece.

Doming and Swaging

The blocks used for doming and swaging are used to form metals into half-spheres and half-cylinders. The blocks, which are made from steel or brass, are available in a range of sizes, and they are used with wooden punches that match the shapes of the blocks.

Shaping
Cut the metal to be shaped to the appropriate size and anneal it. For example, if you want to form a dome of 15mm (about ⅝in) in diameter, cut a circle with a diameter of 17mm (¾in) and place it into the hollow of a dome that has a diameter of 18–20mm (⅞in). Find a punch that fits the hollow but remember to allow for the thickness of the metal being shaped.

Once the dome has been shaped you can bring up the outside edge of the dome so that it will form a neat half-sphere. Punch the dome through a hole drilled in a steel sheet. The entrance side of the hole should be countersunk, and the punch should be able to pass right through the hole, allowing for the extra thickness of the metal dome.

There will be times when you cannot match the punch to the dome. You may, for example, want to make a large domed piece by forming it in a sandbag or on a lead block, or you may have a doming block but only a limited selection of punches. To overcome this problem, place the circle of metal in the block, on the sandbag or on the lead cake, position the punch over it and strike the punch, working first around the outside edge of the metal to begin the shaping process, then gradually working down into the centre in a series of ever-decreasing circles.

When you use lead cake to shape metal, place a piece of cloth or soft leather between the lead and the metal. Any particles of lead that are left on metal during heating melt very quickly and burn holes in the metal, with potentially disastrous results.

Cutting circles
When you need to cut out several circles to the same size, it is tedious to do them all by hand. You can either make a tool to do the job for you or you can buy a tool with a series of different sized holes and matching cutting punches.

Swaging
A swage block is used in exactly the same way as a doming block, but this time you will need to use the handles of your punches, laid

1 Metal doming punches; **2** wooden doming punches; **3** stainless steel swage block – the doming punch handles are used in conjunction with the swage block; **4** stainless steel doming block; **5** leather sandbag used to give a resistant but soft backing.

on their sides, to shape the metal into the hollows of the block. Use a wooden mallet to strike the handles so that they are not marked, or place a flat plate on top for protection.

If your punches do not have handles of the correct size, use a small metal rod to push the edge of the metal into the curve, and gradually work the rod into the centre. Work gently, hitting and pushing, and decrease the size of the rod to prevent "creasing".

SEE ALSO

- Annealing 14–15
- Piercing 100–103

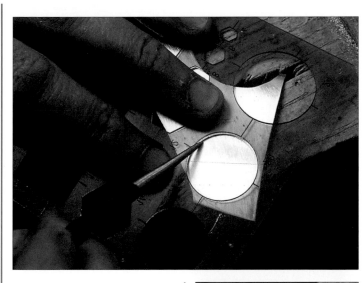

Make a circle cutting tool

To make a circle cutting tool you will need two square blocks, each about 10mm (½in) thick and large enough to accommodate your circle and leave a margin of about 10mm (½in) around the circumference of the circle. Clamp the blocks together and drill a hole to the desired diameter through both. Drill two or four locating holes with a small diameter into the two inside faces of the blocks. These holes do not need to go right through the blocks. Insert locating pins into the base block – they should fit tightly – place a metal washer over each pin and locate the top half of the block over the bottom half. Make the cutter from a steel rod that will fit snugly into the drilled hole. The rod should be 10–12.5cm (4–5in) long, and the top and bottom edges must be completely flat. Place the metal to be cut between the two blocks, centring it under the hole, locate the punch in the top half of the hole and hit it firmly with a hammer.

Doming

1 Scribe a circle with a diameter 1–2mm (¹⁄₁₆in) larger than the diameter of a finished dome.

2 Use a piercing saw to cut around the scribed line. Anneal the metal before doming.

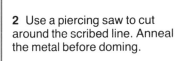

3 Place the circle of metal in the doming block, in a hollow that is slightly larger than the circle. Use a wooden or metal punch that matches the size of the hollow, place the punch over the circle and hit the top of the punch with a hammer or mallet until the dome is formed. This can usually be done with a single blow.

Cutting circles

1 Place the sheet of metal in the block of a cutting-out tool, under the appropriately sized hole.

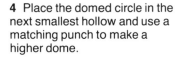

4 Place the domed circle in the next smallest hollow and use a matching punch to make a higher dome.

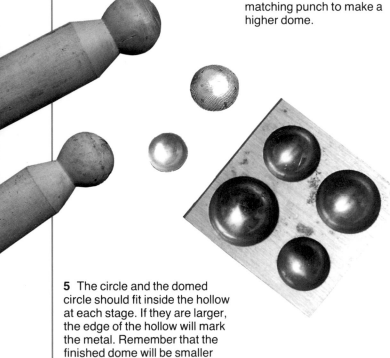

5 The circle and the domed circle should fit inside the hollow at each stage. If they are larger, the edge of the hollow will mark the metal. Remember that the finished dome will be smaller than the original circle.

Making a silver sphere
1 Make a large silver sphere by soldering a domed circle to a silver or copper ring that has a slightly larger diameter. Flatten the edges of the ring and file the bottom edge of the dome to make a neat edge and use hard solder to solder the pieces together.

2 Place the cutter squarely into the hole and hit it sharply with a hammer.

3 The circle will fall through the bottom of the cutting-out tool.

2 File the outside edge so that it is flush with the dome to make it easier to position the second dome correctly. Drill a hole in the centre of the dome.

3 Support the lower section between two charcoal blocks and use medium or easy solder to solder the second dome onto the ring edge. After soldering, drying and cleaning, place the drill through the first hole and drill through to the other side. Drilling the second hole when the bead is assembled ensures that the holes line up.

Swaging
1 Cut a strip of metal that exactly fits into a semicircular slot in the swage block. Match a wooden or metal punch lengthwise along the block, place it on top of the strip of silver and tap along its length with a mallet or hammer.

2 Continue to work in ever-decreasing sizes of slot, annealing the metal if it becomes hard, until you have the curve you want. Do not continue if the metal is too large to fit into the slot.

Making chenier
1 Cut a thin strip of metal and file one end to a point. Place the strip over a swage block so that it just fits into one size slot. Using the handle of a punch, tap the strip down into the slot, and continue until the strip is bent to just over half way. Anneal when necessary to keep the strip soft.

2 Next, place the strip on a flat plate and gently tap down the top edge. Turn the strip over and work along the opposite edge in the same way.

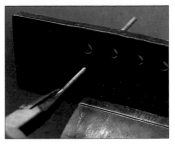

3 When both edges meet, fit the strip into the closest fitting hole in the drawplate. Holding a small blade between the edges just before pulling the strip through the plate will keep the line straight. Continue the process until the correct size is achieved. Anneal after three consecutive pulls.

4 Make a small groove along the join line with a triangular file. Flux along the groove and place paillons of hard solder along it. Carefully solder it up. Mark where the solder join is with a saw blade. The soldered side of chenier should be the side which will be soldered to the parent metal.

Drilling

The most important rule to observe in drilling is to make sure that the hole is drilled where you want it. This is not as simple and obvious as it may sound, and it is worth spending a little time thinking about the position before you begin work.

Marking your position
Always mark the position for the hole before you begin to drill. This can be done with a sprung centre punch, by punching a small mark, or with the point of a scriber. Choose one of the above that is a suitable size for the hole to be drilled and for the thickness of metal.

When using a scriber, hold it firmly on the metal and push downwards with a quick side-to-side motion. If you use a sprung centre punch, lay the piece to be drilled on a flat metal surface, place the centre punch squarely on the metal and push it firmly downwards. The centre punch has a fairly strong action and will usually displace a little of the metal around it, but this is not important if the hole to be drilled is fairly large.

Using a drill
Another element to plan ahead is the stage at which you drill. It is much simpler to drill into a large area of uncut metal than to have to make an accurate hole in a small, neatly cut piece. If you need a centrally positioned hole, it is often easier to drill the hole and then cut the shape around it.

You will need to hold the piece securely while you drill. If the metal can move, it will just spin round with the drill.

Usually, it can be held comfortably in your hand on the pin of the bench, but metal drilled with a bit held in a pendant motor or with an electric pedestal drill can become very hot. In this case, clamp the piece with some wood, which can be held in the hand, or dip the drill into oil and water as you work to keep it cool. It is easier to drill a large hole if you drill a small hole first and then enlarge the hole gradually.

Drilling in a curved surface
Do not try to drill straight into a curved surface because the drill bit will not be able to gain purchase and will slide around and may even break. File a small, flat area on top of the curve, mark the spot to be drilled with a pencil and then mark it firmly with a scriber.

Making a small drill
Small drills can be made from sewing needles. Hold the eye end of the needle in a pair of flat-nosed pliers and snap off the last, pointed one-third with another pair of pliers. Rub the snapped-off end on an oiled carborundum stone, working on opposite sides to create a wedge shape with an angle of about 45 degrees. Lightly smooth away the two opposite corners, which form the sides of the wedge. Drill bits made in this way are very useful and strong, but they are not suitable for drilling metal that is thicker than 1mm (1/32in).

1 Bow drill with cord at correct tension; **2** hand-held pin drill with four different chucks.

①

②

Drilling a hole in flat metal
1 Use a centre punch or a scriber to mark the centre of the hole you wish to drill.

2 Hold the metal in one hand while you make the hole with a small hand drill.

Drilling a hole in a curved surface

Carefully flatten the area you want to drill with a flat needle file. Mark the centre and use a drill held in the pendant motor to make the hole. If you want a slightly larger hole, move the drill in and out of the hole, pushing it gently against the edges to widen the circle.

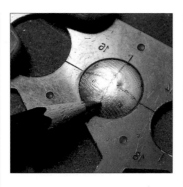

Drilling a hole in a dome
1 Place the dome in a circular template and use a pencil to mark the centre point.

2 Slightly flatten the top with a flat needle file and mark the centre again before drilling through. Use a small hand drill or hold the drill in the chuck of a pendant motor.

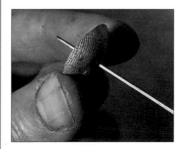

3 Twist a reamer through the hole to enlarge it.

Working on small pieces
When you are drilling through a tiny piece, hold it firmly in a pair of parallel pliers.

Using a bow drill
1 Place your second and third fingers on top of the handle of the bow drill, with your thumb and fourth and fifth fingers positioned under the handle to guide the handle up and down the shaft.

2 The bow will find its own momentum as the tensioned string winds and unwinds around the shaft. It is possible to use very fine drill bits with a bow drill.

Enamelling

Enamelling is a unique and historical way of using colour to enhance your work. Enamels are a mixture of silica, lead oxides, salts of soda, potassium and boric acids, which fuse to a copper, steel, silver or gold surface when they are fired in a kiln.

Enamelling is time consuming. Each stage of the making of the piece has to be related to the enamelling process, and the correct preparation of a piece that is to be enamelled is essential if the results are not to be disappointing.

Type of enamels
Enamels are usually supplied in lump or powder form; they are occasionally found wet mixed. All enamels should be stored in airtight jars. Lump enamels have a longer shelf life than the powdered form, but powdered enamels take less preparation before they are applied to the metal. Enamels supplied in wet mixed form are painted directly onto the metal; they can also be screen printed onto larger areas.

There are three types of enamel: transparent, opaque and opalescent. Transparent enamels depend on the texture or brilliance of the background metal, which is

1 Porcelain mortar and pestle with lump enamel; 2 powdered or ground enamels; 3 transparent lump or frit enamel; 4 unusual Russian lump enamel – the number indicates the colour.

clearly visible, for their own reflective brilliance. Opaque enamels hide the underlying metal, but they have a brilliance of their own. Opalescent enamels have a slightly milky appearance, and some of the background metal is reflected through them. Opalescent enamels have to be fired at very precise temperatures if they are to look their best.

A material known as flux enamel, which can be in either lump or powder form, is frequently used as a first coat or undercoat on standard silver and copper. A transparent flux coat helps the subsequent enamel to retain its colour and brightness in further firings. Fluxes can also be used as an "over-flux" – that is, as the last, clear transparent coat on top of either a transparent or an opaque enamel – to give additional depth to a piece or to "hold" a particular colour that might darken if a further coat of colour were added.

Painting enamels are very finely ground and mixed to a smooth paste with a medium such as lavender oil. They can be painted directly on a metal surface and then covered with a clear flux for firing or, more often, they are painted onto a background of opaque enamels, with the colours being built up slowly over many firings. The final result is similar to a miniature oil or watercolour painting.

Preparing enamels
Before use, enamels must be finely ground, and the water used to wash the grounds must be completely clear before the enamel is transferred to the palette. Any remaining cloudiness will result in a cloudy enamel. Distilled water should be used for the final rinse.

Preparing lump enamels
1 Place lump enamel in the mortar and cover it with water. Hold the pestle directly above the enamel and start to break up the lumps by hitting the top of the pestle with a hammer. Do this until the lumps are small enough to grind.

2 Hold the pestle firmly and use a rotating movement to grind the enamel. Push downwards as you work and continue until the enamel is really fine.

3 The water will be cloudy at this stage. Pour it away carefully, making sure that no ground enamel is lost down the drain.

4 Run more water into the mortar and swill it around with the enamel. Tap the side of the mortar with the pestle to encourage the enamel to settle. Continue to wash the enamel, pouring away and replacing the cloudy water until the water remains clear.

5 Use distilled water for the final rinse because tap water contains impurities that can affect enamel.

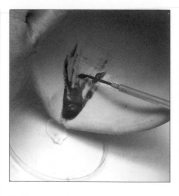

6 Scrape the enamel into a palette or petri dish. It is ready for use.

Placing wet enamels
Because the metal onto which you will be laying the enamels has been thoroughly cleaned, you must take care that it does not become dirty again. Hold the edge between your thumb and forefinger and use a small spatula or the quill end of a feather to scrape a small amount of enamel out of the palette into or on the metal. Spread it out as smoothly as possible so that no metal is visible and the enamel forms an even, fine layer. Gently tap the edge of the piece with the handle of the spatula to help the enamel spread and settle.

If you want to lay a second colour close up against another, dry the first colour by holding the corner of a piece of absorbent tissue to it to draw off the water. When you lay the second colour you may have to let a little water transfer to the first colour, but this will help in the laying. When you have applied a thin coat, the piece must be allowed to dry completely before it is fired. Place it on a wire mesh

support on top of the kiln to dry.

If you are placing colours without a flux base, it is better to fire the different colours at the same time to avoid the firestain that might occur on the exposed silver if only one colour were fired at a time.

Placing Wet Enamels
1 Use a small spatula – a dental spatula is ideal – to place blue flux into the etched-out area.

2 Gently tap the side of the piece with the spatula to encourage the enamel to spread and settle evenly.

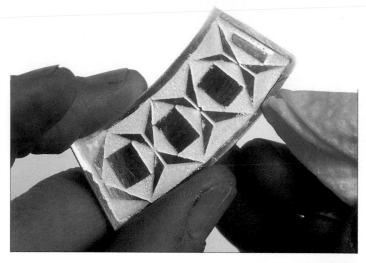

3 Use the corner of an absorbent towel to draw out excess water.

4 When the enamel is dry, hold the piece in the mouth of the kiln for a few seconds to remove all final traces of moisture. Place the piece in the kiln and check after 15–30 seconds. Take the piece from the kiln when the flux has fired to, or just past, the "orange peel" stage.

5 Leave it to cool, then fill the areas with one colour. Because this piece has a base coat of flux, it is easier to fire one colour

first, then apply a second colour and give the piece a second firing. Neaten the edges of the first colour with a moist paintbrush before applying the second colour.

6 Fire the first colour.

7 Fill in the rest of the area with the second colour, remembering to leave it to dry before firing it. Continue to fill in the colours until the enamel is level with, or slightly proud of, the surrounding metal.

Firing enamels

Most enamels are fired at temperatures between 750 and 950°C (1380–1740°F). Hard enamels are fired at the top of the range, while soft enamels are fired at 750–820°C (1380–1500°F). The time taken depends on the size of the piece and the thickness of the metal used.

Hold the enamelled piece at the mouth of the kiln for a moment or two to make sure that the enamel is dry, then place it in the kiln. Remove the piece as soon as it has a slightly "orange peel" appearance.

Leave it to cool on a rack near to the kiln.

When the piece is cool, apply a second coat of enamel and fire as before. The enamel should look smooth and glossy after the initial firing.

Apply several thin layers of enamel rather than one or two thick ones. This will allow you to control the colour and makes cracking less likely.

Articles to be enamelled should be placed on steel supports or on wire mesh trays, which you should place in and take out of the kiln with a long firing fork. Protect your hand with a protective glove.

Counter enamel

As enamels are fired onto the front of a piece of metal, stresses build up in the metal that, unless balanced, will force the metal to curve towards the centre of the enamel. This can be prevented by applying a coat of enamel, known as counter enamel, to the back of the piece. The counter enamel is applied either before or after the first coat of enamel is applied to the front.

Counter enamel can spoil the appearance of the back of a piece. This can be overcome by setting the enamel piece as you would a stone so that the back is hidden. Alternatively, the metal used for the piece could

be thicker than would normally be the case to prevent it from curving – for example, if the depth of the enamel for a piece of champlevé enamel was 0.3mm, the silver could be 1.3mm thick.

The kiln

Kilns can be either electric or gas-fired, and they range in size from 11 x 11 x 6cm (4 x 4 x 2½in) to 26 x 26 x 12cm (10 x 10 x 5in). A gas-fired kiln, which can run on natural or propane gas, is quick to reach the required temperature and, because the heat is reducing rather than reflective, metal is slightly less prone to oxidization. Most gas-fired kilns have a regulator or a pyrometer.

Electric kilns take longer to heat up. They can be fitted with either a regulator on a 1–10 dial or with a pyrometer, which shows the exact temperature of the kiln.

If your kiln has neither a regulator nor a pyrometer, you will be able to assess the approximate temperature by the colour, and when it gets too hot for firing, turn it off for 5 minutes until the temperature has fallen to the correct level.

Applying painting enamels

Place a small amount of powdered painting enamel on a glass tile about 10 x 10cm (4 x 4in) next to a few drops of lavender oil and use a flat spatula to draw the oil into the powder. Press down the mixture to make a smooth paste.

Apply the enamel with a fine sable paintbrush. When you are painting onto opaque enamel, rub the surface of the enamel slightly with wet and dry papers to make a matt surface. Build up the colours

gradually. You will find that at first they tend to fade into the background, and soft colours – red, for example – should be left until all the hard firings have been completed and the temperature of the kiln can be lowered.

Painting enamels, lustres and lining enamels must all be absolutely dry before firing. Leave them on top of the kiln until the paint looks whitish, then hold them at the mouth of the kiln so that any remaining oil evaporates.

Place the piece in the kiln and remove it when the painted enamels gloss. These enamels fire quicker than ground enamels. As the picture is built up and more colours are added, the piece will have to be fired several times. Painted enamels are usually covered with a soft over-glaze flux, which not only gives a protective coating but also helps to create a sense of depth.

Preparing the metal

Metal that is to be enamelled must be scrupulously clean. Any soldering must be completed before enamelling starts, and if hard enamels are being used you might use enamelling solder; otherwise, use hard solder. After annealing or soldering, the piece must be cleaned. Hold it under running water and rub it all over with a glass brush until the water stays smoothly all over the surface instead of running into globules. Keep it in distilled water until you are ready to begin enamelling, when it can be dried on a paper towel and then licked – yes, licked – to make sure it is perfectly clean and neutral.

Colour Temperature Guide	
Dull red	720°C+ (1330°F)
Dull orange-red	750°C (1380°F)
Cherry red	790°C+ (1450°F)
Bright red-orange	820°C+ (1500°F)
Very bright orange	870–1000°C (1600–1830°F)

Preparing the metal

1 A sheet of silver has been photoetched and is being prepared for enamelling. Pierce out the individual shape to be enamelled from the sheet.

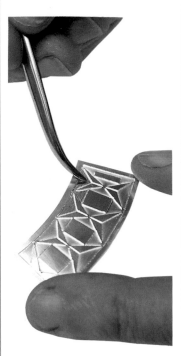

2 Hold the metal under running water and clean it with a glass brush.

3 Make the background even more reflective by using a burnisher.

When plain metal is to be enamelled, it must be completely free of grease and oxides. Use a glass brush under running water until the water stays smoothly over the surface.

Use an engraving tool to give the metal a reflective texture, and remove any remaining bits of solder with a straight-edged engraver.

Finishing a piece

When you have applied the correct amount of enamel and it is level with the cloisons or metal surrounds, the enamel must be smoothed and refired to give a neat, flat surface. When it is cool, hold the piece under running water and rub a fine carborundum stone to and fro over it until the enamel is level. Grades 280–400 of wet and dry paper can be used under running water to give a finer finish. Dry the piece and check that the enamel is smooth. Any low areas can be filled with the appropriate colour and the piece refired. If the refilled areas need smoothing down, this is done now so that the enamel is completely level for the final "flash firing", which should be done at a slightly higher temperature and more quickly than previous firings.

Enamels can also be left matt, which means that they do not need the final flash firing after rubbing down with fine wet and dry papers.

Test piece

Always fire a test piece first. Use a piece of properly prepared silver, and try firing your selected colours at different temperatures. Watch to see how and when each one fires and, from the results, work out the order of firing the piece. It is a good idea to keep the results of each of your samples as a reference. Fire colours direct onto silver and on top of a clear flux, and onto silver and gold foil to assess whether you need to use flux on your piece.

2 Dry the piece and check to see if more depressions need to be filled. If necessary, fill and refire before rubbing down as before. Place the piece in the kiln for flash firing.

Finishing a piece

1 When it is cool, hold the piece under running water and rub it level with a carborundum stone, which is rubbed horizontally across the piece until the enamel is level. Use wet and dry papers, wrapped around the carborundum stone, still with the piece under running water.

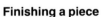

Test sample

Carrying out tests is one of the most important aspects of enamelling. You are aiming to discover how the enamel reacts to different effects. This test sample shows the effects of different firing times, temperatures, acid and polishes.

Enamelling techniques

There are approximately seven different types of enamelling technique, including painting.

En bosse ronde Apply enamel directly to the surface of the metal, which can be flat, domed or repoussé.

Champlevé This French word means "level field", which is exactly what the enamel becomes when it has been applied in layers until it is level with the surrounding metal.

Depressions in the metal are made by etching, photoetching, engraving or chiselling, or by soldering a pierced sheet about 0.4mm thick onto a solid sheet of the same metal that is at least twice as thick. Thin layers of enamel are placed in the depressions until they are just above the surface of the metal. The enamel is then stoned to the level of the metal before flash firing.

Cloisonné The word *cloison* is French for "cell", and in this technique cells are made by bending flattened cloisonné wire to make a pattern, either to fit depressions, as in champlevé, or to be placed directly on the metal as in en bosse ronde.

The wires can be soldered to the metal, but you must be careful not to let any solder show through transparent enamel. It is more usual to fire a layer of flux first, place the bent cloisonné wires on the flux, holding them in position with a little Klyrfyre Glue, and then fire them in place. The wire should be as fine as possible because thick cloisonné wire can look heavy and unattractive.

The cloisons are filled with enamel, as in champlevé, but take care not to rub down the cloisonné wire enamel too soon. Little pieces of wire may get embedded in the enamel, and they will be difficult to remove.

2 Flatten the sides of the wire slightly by passing it through a rolling mill. The wire stands on edge, so try to make sure that the height is fractionally greater then the etched depth of the metal. Apply a base coat of flux.

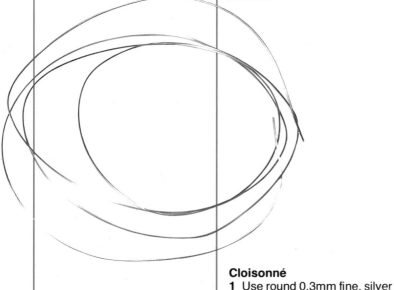

Cloisonné
1 Use round 0.3mm fine, silver cloisonné wire.

3 Use round-nosed pliers and fine stainless steel tweezers to bend the cloisonné wire accurately. Keep a drawing or pattern of the design to hand so that you can measure the wires accurately and shape them carefully before dipping each piece in a little Klyfyre and placing it in position. The Klyrfyre will hold the wires in place until the piece is fired.

4 When the wires are in position, put the piece on a mesh tray and place it in the kiln. Fire until the flux starts to gloss and wires sink into it.

5 Any wires that do not sink into the flux can be gently pushed down with the side of a burnisher.

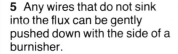

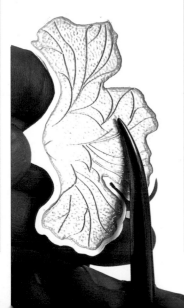

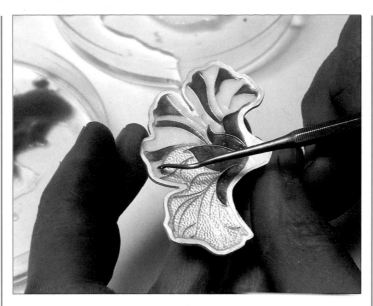

6 The separate colours can now be placed in the cloisons. If any colour strays into the neighbouring cloison lift it away with the tip of a moistened paintbrush. It is easier to remove it now than later on.

7 Leave the piece on the top of the kiln to dry. Before you put it in the kiln, make sure that no foreign bodies have landed on the enamels. Carefully lift out any specks with the tip of the paintbrush.

8 After the layers have been applied and individually fired, the final layer should be fractionally higher than the edge of the piece. Rub it with a carborundum stone under running water before giving a final flash firing.

Plique à jour In this technique the enamel has no metal backing. A pattern is usually pierced out or it can be made by soldering cloisonné wires into the desired pattern. The wet enamel is placed in the holes and is held there by capillary action. The holes should be no larger than 1cm (⅓in) square, and you should avoid sharp corners because the enamel will not adhere well. The pattern is either supported on steel supports or laid flat on a piece of mica.

Basse taille The French words mean "deep cut" and refer to surface decoration of the metal before transparent enamels are applied. The decoration is usually engraved, and different tones of colour are achieved by altering the depths of the lines of the engraving. Transparent colours can be applied and merged according to the pattern beneath.

Grisaille This technique uses only black and white. The base coat is usually black onto which white is built up in several layers. The white enamels gradually blend into the black, creating various tones of dark and light grey and white.

Gold and silver foils Foil can be applied under transparent and opalescent enamel to give a brilliantly reflective background. The gold foil brings out the true colours of the enamels and, in addition to the reflection, silver foil can be useful if you are having trouble with firestain on silver.

Engraving

Engraving is the art of removing surface metal to create a decoration. Much of the finely worked silver and gold that is seen is the work of highly skilled professional engravers, who use techniques and practices acquired over many years. However, most jewellery makers can learn the rudiments of engraving, and it can be used to good effect in a variety of ways.

The tools
The cutting edges most often used in engraving are:
- Lozenge – for lines
- Square or diamond – for lines
- Dotter or round
- Square scorper – for removing metal
- Spitstick – for cleaning up edges
- Chisel
- Liner – for making background channels

The steel engraving tool is made or bought separately from the handle, and can be made to the appropriate shape and length to suit individual needs. For example, straight gravers are suitable for working on flat or convex surfaces, while angled or curved ones are better for working on concave or repousséd surface. See Stamping and Blanking (pages 116–121) for making steel tools.

The handles are made from wood and can be either round or have one flat side, which makes it possible to hold the tool almost level with the work.

Always keep the cutting edge crisp and sharp. The belly of the tool – that is, the area where it meets the cutting edge can be rubbed back to a slight angle with a stone to prevent drag lines being made on the metal. If necessary, the tool can be shortened by holding it in a vice and snapping off the shaft.

Holding the work
Work that is to be engraved must be held steady and flat, but you also need to be able to turn it freely as you work. There are several options. Work can be held in a wooden vice that is itself held on a revolving sandbag, or it can be held in the pitch bowl, which you can turn by hand. If you are working on a small, flat piece, an engraver's hand-held vice is useful. The piece is held by pins that can be located in any of the holes covering the surface of the vice.

Other pieces can be placed on the pin on the bench and held by hand. Hold the work between your thumb and forefinger so that you can make a smooth movement when the work has to be turned. Take care to keep your fingers out of the line of the engraving tool. If it slips you may cut your fingers badly. Holding work by hand can be quite tiring, so if you are working on a complex piece that will take some time to complete, try to find another way.

Holding the tool
The wooden handle of the tool should sit comfortably in the palm of your hand. Your forefinger should extend so that it lies along the top of the tool, and the thumb of the hand holding the tool should rest on the surface of the metal

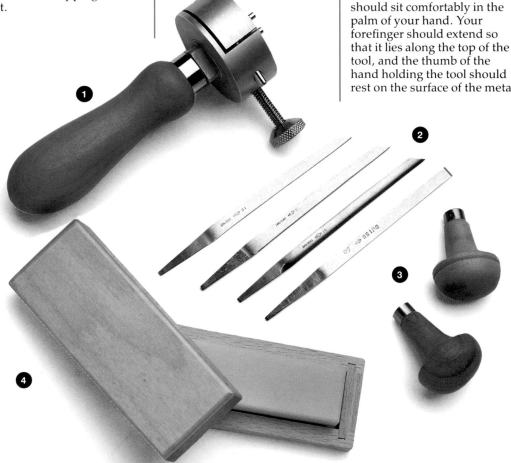

being engraved or on the medium in which it is being held. This thumb acts as a guide and a brake and sometimes as a pivot.

Cutting

Select a tool that is the correct shape for the cut to be made. It must be sharpened on a stone to an angle of 45 degrees. If it is less than 45 degrees, the tip will be too long and may snap. If it is more than 45 degrees, it is more difficult to work and tends to dig into the metal.

To start a cut on a straight line, hold the tool almost vertically so that it gets some purchase in the metal, then quickly lower it so that your thumb can be placed horizontally on the work. Push the tool along the line to raise a tiny curl of metal, then flick up the tool to remove the sliver. Continue in this way along the line.

Curved lines are made with a tool that has been stoned away on one side edge. Turn the work smoothly as the line is being cut – the hand that is

holding the tool should remain in more or less the same position while the work is turned beneath it.

When engraving is used to remove areas of metal, the area should be outlined with a lozenge chisel and then a second line, approximately 1mm (1/32in) inside the first, should be cut. The area within the second line is then removed with a square scorper or chisel. The base can then be engraved with a lined tool and the edges cut away with a smaller square scorper before being cleaned up with a spitstick.

Sharpening the graver

Use a fine carborundum stone or an Arkansas stone to sharpen your engraving tools. Put a small amount of oil on the stone and hold the tool flat on its face at an angle of 45 degrees from the stone. Rub the tool along the stone, to and fro, making sure that the whole face remains in contact with the top of the stone. Turn over the tool and rub the stone square along the belly or hold it at an angle if you want to smooth away part of the belly. If the side needs to be shaped or sharpened hold it at the correct angle and rub in a circular motion.

1 Engraver's vice – adjustable hand-held vice which holds varying sizes of metal to be engraved; 2 four assorted gravers; 3 flat-sided handles; 4 Arkansas sharpening stone, which should be used with oil.

Preparing the tools
1 Line up the bottom edge of the engraving tool with the flat side of the handle.

2 Hold the tool in the safe jaws of the vice and use a mallet to hammer down the handle on to it.

3 Put a little oil on the stone and sharpen the graver by rubbing it straight along its cutting angle.

SEE ALSO

• Stamping & making blanks 116–121

61

4 Use a chisel-end tool to dig out a little edge up to the main line of the pattern.

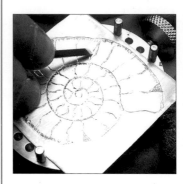

5 Use the lozenge tool for the pattern. Here it is being used to cross-hatch shaded areas.

Engraving a design

1 Rub the surface of the metal with putty and then trace it through to transfer the design to be engraved to the surface of the metal; make sure that the lines are clear and easy to follow.

2 Follow the line with a lozenge engraving tool. Remove small slivers and flick up the tool to clear away the sliver.

3 When you need to turn to the left or right, grind the edge of the tool so that it naturally turns that way.

6 Unintentional slips with the graver can be disguised by dropping a spot of oil on the area and rubbing along the scratch with a polished burnisher. Keep the burnisher low so that it straddles the line and do not rub across the line, as it will accentuate the error.

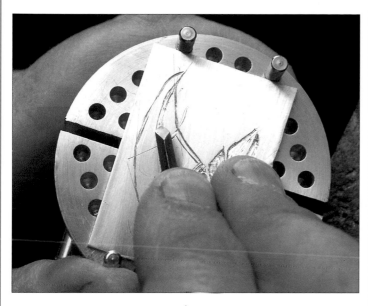

Removing metal for inlay or enamel

1 To remove metal for inlay or enamel, outline the pattern with a lozenge tool then engrave another line close to the first.

2 Remove the area within this second line with a chisel-type tool.

3 Use a flat-faced tool to level the base of this area. Press some Plasticine down into the areas from which you have removed the metal to check that it is perfectly level.

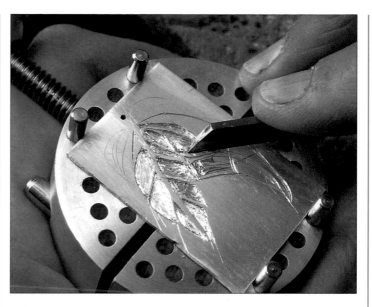

4 Remove the edges up to the first line.

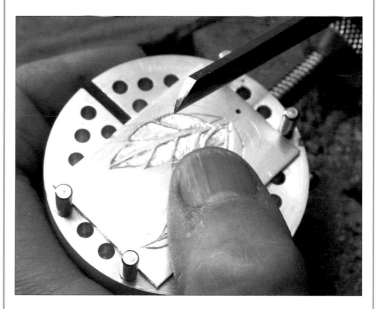

5 Clean up all the edges with a spitstick.

Etching and Photoetching

Etching

Etching has many uses in jewellery making, and it is a quick and relatively easy process. The aim is to use an acid solution, known as a mordant, to eat or dissolve away exposed sections of metal. You can obtain different depths, depending on how long the metal stays in the mordant. If a decorative surface is required, the depth of etch need not be very great. If, however, the depression is to be used for enamelling or for laying in resins, the etch will need to be deeper – between 0.3 and 0.5mm deep.

Always remember that the acids used in etching can be dangerous. Always handle them carefully and sensibly. Keep them in clearly labelled containers and store them in a locked cupboard.

Types of resist

A resist is a substance that protects the surface of the metal against the active properties in the mordant. The most common resist is called **"stop-out" varnish,** which is a thickish bitumen-based liquid painted directly onto all areas on the metal that need to be protected. Support the work on a little stand so that you can apply the varnish without

having to touch the metal, and when the front is dry, turn it over and paint the other side. Remember to paint all edges with the varnish. Any tidying up, such as straightening wobbly lines, can be done when the varnish is dry by drawing the edge of a sharp blade down the line and gently lifting or scraping away excess varnish.

Make sure that the varnish is completely dry before placing the piece in the etching fluid.

An alternative resist to varnish is **beeswax.** Melt the wax into a small tin, warm the metal and dip it in the wax, which will coat the metal in a thin, even layer. When the wax is cool, cut or draw the pattern through it.

If you want a decorative or pictorial effect on metal, you can use a **hard or a soft ground** "stop-out". This is a mixture of beeswax, bitumen and rosin, and it is applied to the warmed

metal with either a leather dabber or a fine cloth bag containing the ground. The ground is spread evenly over the metal with a small roller. Hard ground is then treated in the smoky end of a candle flame, which is played over the "stop-out" until it goes dark. When the ground is cool, the picture or pattern can be drawn through it with the tip of a tapestry needle or a special etching needle. A coat of ordinary "stop-out" is then painted over the sides and underside of the metal.

Preparing the metal

Before you apply the resist (see below), the metal must be cleaned thoroughly with pumice powder paste or by rubbing with wet and dry papers under running water. If the metal is not completely clean the varnish will lift when it is left in the mordant, exposing the metal that you wanted to protect.

Depending on the intricacy of the design, the pattern is

1 sheet of cleaned silver;
2 tracing paper and pencils for transferring the design;
3 scribe for marking through beeswax.

transferred to the metal either before or after it is cleaned. If the design is complex, rub the surface of the metal with putty or plasticine and trace the design onto it. Remove the tracing paper and scribe through the lines with a sharp metal point. Then clean the metal thoroughly. For a free-form design, clean the metal first, then draw on the design with a sharp lead pencil, but take care not to touch the metal with your fingers.

Preparing the etching fluid

You will need to make up solutions of different strengths according to the metal you are going to etch.
Copper
1 part nitric acid, 1 part water **or** 2 parts potassium chloride, 10 parts hydrochloric acid, 90 parts water.

Silver

3 parts water, 1 part nitric acid **or, for a longer, slower etch** 5 or 6 parts water, 1 part nitric acid.

Gold – 18, 14 and 9 carat

8 parts hydrochloric acid, 4 parts nitric acid, 1 part iron perchloride, 40 or 50 parts water (aqua regia) **or** 2 parts nitric acid, 2 parts sulphuric (or hydrochloric) acid, 4 parts water. Gold will not dissolve in the etching fluid for silver or copper.

Using the etching fluid

Mix up the mordant or buy it ready mixed.

When you are working with etching fluid, always wear, in addition to protective gloves, safety glasses and an apron. Work in a well-ventilated area because the acids will give off strong fumes. Mix sufficient mordant to cover the piece, but do not mix more than you need. An ovenproof glass bowl is suitable for all these mordants.

Use stainless steel or plastic tweezers to place the piece of metal in the mordant, then watch the reaction of the fluid on the exposed metal. If it is too violent – that is, if a lot of bubbles rise quickly to the surface – the mordant may be too strong. Dilute it by putting 1 or 2 parts of water in another dish and carefully transferring the mordant to the new bowl. Generally, the etch will take between 15 and 30 minutes, depending on the strength of the mordant and the depth required. If you are doing a very long, gentle etch, the metal may need to be in the mordant for 3 hours.

In addition to etching downwards, the mordant bites sideways into the metal, once it has penetrated beneath the "stop-out". A slow etch helps to overcome this problem to some extent, but you should take this "undercutting" into account when you prepare the design, because it can result in some fine lines becoming rather ragged.

To test the depth of the etch, remove the metal from the mordant, then rinse and dry. Run the fine point of a steel scriber over the surface and into the etched areas to get a feel for the depth achieved thus far. If the piece needs further etching, check to see if the "stop-out" needs retouching. If it does, remove any flakes of varnish, dry thoroughly and lift any raised areas with the blade of a craft knife. Repaint the area or areas with varnish and make sure it is completely dry before returning it to the mordant.

Cleaning and finishing

When you are satisfied with the depth of the etch, remove the piece from the mordant and rinse it thoroughly under running water. Store the etching fluid in a clearly labelled glass jar or put a lid on the bowl. Although mordant can be re-used, it will turn a clear deep blue-green when spent. When this happens, dilute it with as much water as possible and dispose of it, again in running water.

Dry the washed metal with

1 Stop-out varnish with paintbrushes; **2** warmed beeswax for coating the silver; **3** nitric acid solution for etching.

paper towel before either wiping it with white spirit or turpentine or leaving it in a shallow bath of turpentine. Remove a beeswax "stop-out" by holding the piece over the tin of wax and heating it with a gentle flame so that the wax drips back into the tin.

When all traces of "stop-out" have been removed, clean the piece with pumice powder paste, which can be applied with a toothbrush. Neaten any ragged lines with a "spitstick" engraving tool. If the piece is to be enamelled, rub all over the etched area with a glass-fibre brush and then use a polished burnisher to brighten the area.

Photoetching

This process, which is generally carried out by commercial firms, is particularly suitable for work that is to be enamelled or that involves a lot of intricate piercing of several pieces. Photoetching involves photosensitizing metals to produce a "resist" and to print an image that can then be attacked by a suitable etching fluid. When it is used to make jewellery, photoetching is an extremely accurate process, as long as a number of guidelines are observed.

Most photoetching firms prefer to work on a sheet of metal that is not smaller than about 45 x 30cm (18 x 12in), so the design needs to be carefully considered and the number of items required needs planning to fit into the area. The etch can then be taken to an accurate depth, and if the sheet is no thicker than 1mm ($\frac{1}{32}$in), the etch can pierce through the metal for either decorative purposes or to save piercing out the item later.

When you are designing for

photoetching, the image should be drawn and painted to about twice the size of the finished piece. The final artwork can be reduced to half size, either by photocopying or by the grid method. The solid, coloured area represents the metal that is going to be etched away.

When you present the finished design to the photoetching firm, remember that:

- The design should fit on a sheet about 45 x 30cm (18 x 12in), with a margin of about 2.5cm (1in) all round.
- The areas to be etched should be shown in solid red, and the depth of the etch required noted in writing.
- Areas to be pierced through should be shown as solid black lines.
- If you are using black lines for areas to be pierced, make sure that the metal is no more than 1mm (1/32in) thick.
- If you are assembling a design from several sections, make sure that you white out all the edges, so that they do not photograph as black lines.
- Use the sheet of metal as economically as you can. It is rather wasteful if you get only two or three pieces from one sheet.

SEE ALSO

- Annealing 14—15
- Pickling & quenching 98—99
- Polishing 104—105

2 Mix pumice powder to a paste and use an old toothbrush to rub it all over the metal. Rinse thoroughly under running water until the water stays all over the surface. If the water forms little globules, the metal is not sufficiently clean.

Preparing the metal for etching
1 Thoroughly clean the metal with grade 280—400 wet and dry paper, holding it under running water.

3 Use a pencil to draw the pattern on the clean silver, making sure that your fingers do not touch any of the areas to be etched.

Using the resist
1 Paint a coat of "stop out" over the areas you do not want to be etched and leave to dry.

2 When the front is dry, turn over the piece and place it on a stand so that you can coat the back and edges with "stop out" varnish. Leave to dry.

Using the etching fluid
1 Place the piece in the nitric acid solution and watch for bubbles to rise. To achieve an even etch, use a feather to remove the bubbles as they form.

Cleaning and finishing
Pierce around the outside lines of the pattern.

2 When the required depth is achieved, remove the piece from the acid and rinse it under water. Remove the "stop out" varnish by soaking or cleaning with a rag soaked in turpentine.

Safety Precautions

Remember that you should always add acid to water. **Never add water to acid,** because it may bubble and foam rapidly in the container and even spill over the top. Always wear protective gloves, and if any acid is spilled, douse the affected area with plenty of water to dilute it and mop it up with an old cloth.

Filing

The purpose of filing is to remove excess metal. Jewellery makers use different grades of file to achieve different finishes, but large escapement and engineering files are not suitable for delicate jewellery. Filing is also the first step towards finishing a piece, and it is important that you should use the files in the correct sequence, so that any marks made by one are removed by the next. The finished article should not bear any file marks. You should always take great care when filing – it is impossible to replace the metal removed by each stroke of a file.

Files are graded by the coarseness of the cut. A "zero" or 0 file is the coarsest, 2 gives a medium cut, and 4 is the finest. Some needle files are graded down to 6. If quite a large amount of metal has to be removed, a large 0 file will do

1 Large flat file; **2** large oval file; **3** needle files; **4** riffler files, designed to reach inside awkward places and useful for filing inside little holes between twisted wires, and in convex and concave areas, and for removing traces of solder.

the work most efficiently, but any further filing should be done with a finer grade and this should be followed by an even finer needle file.

Choose a correctly shaped file for each job. On an inside curve you should use an oval or a half-round file. If you need a crisp right angle, use a square file. Grooves are best worked with a triangular file. A groove for chenier can be filed with either a round file or a joint round-edge file. Some files have "safe" edges, so if you need to file close to an area that you do not want to mark, you can work with the "safe" area next to the area to be protected.

Using files

When you use a file it is important to keep the direction level. For example, if you are straightening a line, use a flat file and keep it absolutely parallel to the line. If you do not, the corners at the ends of the line will tend to curve and drop below the line.

Files usually cut in only one direction, so place the article on the bench pin and hold it steady with one hand while you hold the file in the other hand, and then work with a forward cutting movement. Rubbing a file backwards and forwards over a piece is ineffective.

Using wet and dry papers

After filing you should clean the area with wet and dry papers. These are available in grades ranging from 240, through 400 and 600, to 1200, and you should keep a variety of grades in your workshop so that you can work through each grade if you want a highly polished finish. As their name suggests, these papers can be used with or without water. Water helps to keep the surface smooth by washing away the metal particles as they are removed by the paper. When you are sitting at your work area, however, it is often impracticable to have a bowl of water in front of you and water dripping on the bench. The papers are, therefore, often used dry.

When you are rubbing down

a flat metal surface with wet and dry papers, place the paper on a flat surface – an old tile or a piece of mirror, for example, or a metal flat plate – and rub the work along it.

Making an emery board

Small sections of paper can be cut from a large sheet and wrapped around a file to remove file marks. Papers can also be glued to wooden sticks. Take a small piece of wood, approximately 200 x 20 x 5mm (8 x 2 x ¼in), and glue a section of wet and dry paper, about 130 x 50mm (5 x 2in), around one end of the stick. The wood creates a firm, flat base that can be drawn across the metal. This is used dry.

Burnishing

A burnisher is a highly polished, hard steel tool that is rubbed firmly backwards and forwards on metal to create a polished, shiny surface.

A curved burnisher can be used to polish the top edge of the bezel for a cabochon stone setting. This is a delicate operation, but you do need to

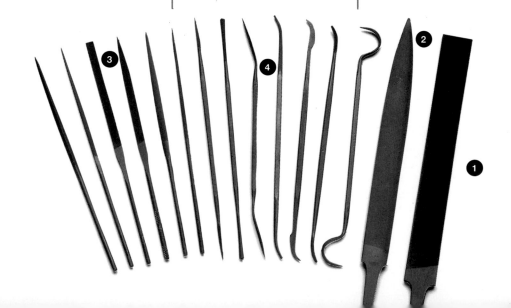

exert quite a lot of pressure on a burnisher to polish a surface and it is easy to slip and damage the stone, especially a soft stone such as an opal, which could crack under sudden pressure. Use your other hand as a brake on the burnisher to avoid damaging the stone.

Use your burnisher to remove scratches caused by slips of engraving tools or other little mishaps. Put a drop of oil on the affected area and rub the burnisher sideways, along the direction of the scratch. If you rub the burnisher across the direction of the scratch you may make it worse. Finish off with fine wet and dry paper, again working in the same direction as you smooth over the burnished area.

2 When you file a curved surface with a flat file, use stroking, upward movements. On the ring, for example, the file is moved against the curve of the metal and the ring is moved around so that the file covers the whole surface.

4 Flatten uneven edges of a ring by rubbing it on a broad flat file, held steady on a flat surface.

Making a chamfered edge
1 Use a pair of dividers to draw a line 1–2mm (1/16in) from the top edge of the ring.

Using files
1 When you file a straight edge, keep the file level by balancing it with your non-working hand. Cut across the edge at a slight angle, rather than directly across it, and make sure that you do not drop the file at the ends of the piece of metal.

3 Use an oval file on the bottom curve of the inside of a ring, working with sweeping movements. Turn the ring around so that the file can make the same movement but from the other side. Always take care that you do not file away too much metal, especially around a soldered join.

5 Use a round needle file to tidy up the inside surface of a ring.

2 Hold a broad flat file at an angle of 45 degrees, working around the edge down to the line marked in step 1. Remove the marks made by the large flat file with a flat needle file and clean the edge thoroughly with wet and dry paper before polishing.

Filing other surfaces
1 Use a three-cornered or square file to make a groove in metal that is to be bent to a right angle. Begin the groove with a scriber or by making a cut with a saw blade. Use the file only when the line has been established.

2 A riffler file can be used to remove paillons of solder from areas that other files cannot reach.

Finishing off filed surfaces
1 When a flat edge is required on a flat surface use wet and dry paper to clean the area.

3 Wrap wet and dry paper around an oval needle file and, working with the same sweeping movement, clean away the marks left by the needle file.

3 Riffler files are available in various shapes. This one is used to clean up a cast ring.

2 Emery boards can be used to clean up flat surfaces.

4 Use a burnisher to give polished highlights to edges and raised areas. Keep the burnisher highly polished for best results.

Fittings and Findings

Most pieces of jewellery need an attachment of some kind that allows them to be worn. When made by hand, they are called fittings, when bought ready made, they are called findings.

Fittings can be made as an integral part of a piece of jewellery. For example, a pendant can be made with an area for hanging around the neck as part of the overall pattern or a pin can be made as an extension of a brooch.

Soldering
If a fitting or finding is an extra piece that needs to be soldered to the article, this is usually done after all the main work has been completed.

Carefully mark the position of the fitting or finding, then position yourself in such a way that you can clearly see your mark and that you are placing the fitting or finding correctly. Paint a little flux on the spot on which the finding will sit and place a paillon of solder in the flux. Paint the base of the fitting with flux and, if you think it will be necessary, run a little solder on the base of the fitting before you begin.

Attaching fittings
A pendant attachment is placed on the charcoal block, close to the pendant. Flux the join, making sure the contact is good, and if it moves while you are heating it, push it back into position with insulated tweezers before the solder flows.

Assembly
Riveted parts of a fitting should always be assembled after all soldering is completed. For example, a pin of a brooch should not be attached until all the other parts of the brooch have been completed, the T-bars of a pair of cuff links should be riveted only when all other work has been completed, and the clips on clip-on earrings should be riveted or sprung into place only when the rest of the work is finished. If these findings are assembled before the soldering is completed, they would become annealed and lose their springiness.

Positioning
The balance of a piece depends on the position of the fitting. On a brooch, for instance, the sitting of the fichu joint and catch is crucial. You also need to consider the way in which a brooch will hang when it is pinned to a garment – will it sit comfortably or flop forwards or sideways? The brooch pin will grip more firmly if the catch is set off line of the fichu joint.

If you are making cuff links with a T-bar, check that the alignment is correct before soldering. When you make a chain link, make sure that it is long enough to wear comfortably but not so long that it does not do its job. Use an odd number of links between the two back faces so that they sit properly.

Earring fittings also need careful positioning. The weight of a piece will affect the position of the post on the back of an ear stud. A heavy stud will flop forwards, and to avoid this the post should be placed close to the top of the stud.

SEE ALSO

- Drilling 50—51
- Piercing 100—103
- Riveting 108—111
- Soldering 112—115

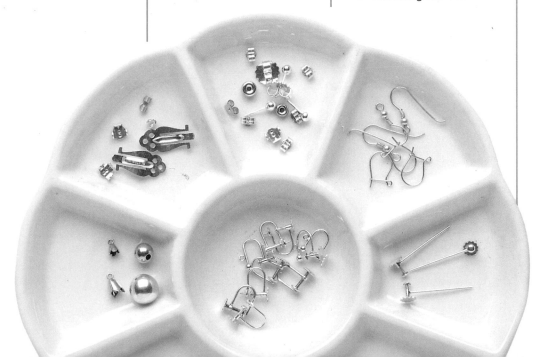

A selection of ready-made silver findings.

Attaching earring fittings

1 Use a pair of insulated tweezers to hold the post steady when you solder it to the back of the earring. Allow the solder to begin to flow before placing the post in it, then take away the flame and hold the post in place until the solder is completely hard. Quench, pickle, rinse and dry.

Making brooch fittings

1 Cut a strip of metal approximately 4 x 10mm (³/₁₆ x ½in) and score a line about 4mm (³/₁₆in) in from each short end. File along the lines until the grooves are just deeper than half the thickness of the metal. Mark the centre of the end sections.

3 Use a three-sided needle file to make a small groove in the top of the joint in which the pin will sit.

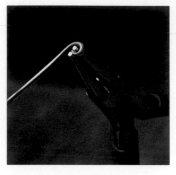

4 With the flat side of the wire on the inside of the curve, bend a strip of D-section wire into the shape of a small "e". Cut the end of the wire with a piercing saw and file the bottom flat so that it will stand on the back of the brooch before it is soldered in place.

2 Hold the base of the earring steady and allow the solder to begin to flow before placing the fitting onto it. Make sure the clip is correctly positioned before you remove the flame. Hold the clip steady for a few seconds before quenching. Solder a screw fitting to the earring before you bend it up. After cleaning and polishing the earring, use a pair of half-round pliers to bend the screw fitting into a smooth curve.

2 Drill a hole in the centre of each of the end sections and bend up the strip along the grooves until the sides are parallel.

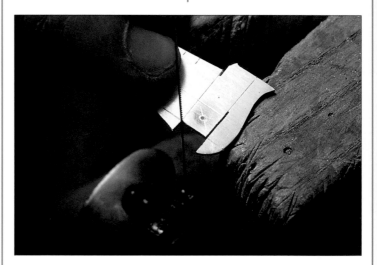

5 Make the tab for the pin by marking the centre of a square about 4 x 4mm (³/₁₆ x ³/₁₆in) and drilling a hole at this point. Use a piercing saw to cut out the square.

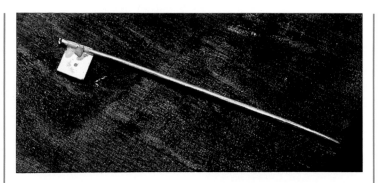

6 File a small groove in the top of the tab into which the pin will fit, and solder the two pieces together with easy solder. At this stage the pin should extend beyond the end of the tab; it can be neatened later. Solder the pin and tab together.

Making a hinged pin joint

1 A hinge joint is used for the pin on a larger brooch. Cut out a square approximately 7 x 7mm (⅜ x ⅜in), file a groove 2mm (¹⁄₁₆in) in from one edge and bend up the edge at a right angle. Cut two pieces of chenier with an outside diameter of 1.2mm (¹⁄₃₂in), which will sit in the angle. Solder them in place and neaten the edges with a flat file.

3 Flatten the end of a piece of wire for the hinge end of the pin.

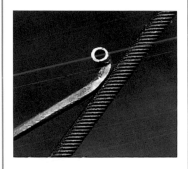

4 Cut a piece of chenier to fit snugly between the two pieces already soldered into position and solder it to the flattened end of the pin. Neaten the edges with a file.

7 After soldering, make the pin springy by rolling it along the steel flat bed, tapping it with a flat hammer as you do so.

8 The fichu joint and catch should not be directly in line with each other. File the tab of the pin so that it fits neatly into the fichu joint and can move easily.

9 Make a simple pin by bending round the end of a piece of wire that is thick enough to fit snugly into the fichu joint. The rivet pin passes through the joint, through the bent wire and out at the other side.

5 Thread a length of wire that will fit through the chenier through the three hinge sections and rivet the ends to hold the pin in place.

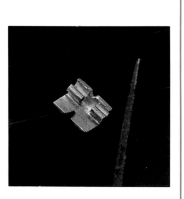

2 File a groove in the centre of the top edge to accommodate the pin.

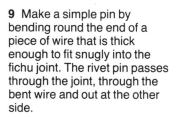

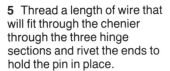

2 Attach the fitting to the back of the cuff link, using hard or medium solder.

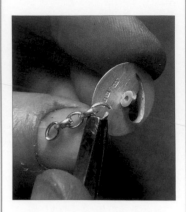

3 Take five or seven sections of chain and pierce open the two end sections. Attach the link to the fitting and isolate it before closing the join with easy solder.

Attaching cuff link fittings
Run solder onto the back of the cuff link. Hold the fitting in insulated tweezers and hold it squarely in place as the solder flows. Remove the flame and hold the fitting steady for a few seconds before quenching.

Clean and finish the cuff link before riveting the T-bar in place.

Making chain link fittings
1 Drill a hole about 2mm (1/16in) from the straight edge of a piece of silver. Scribe a line around the outside of the hole, leaving the bottom edge flat, and pierce around the line. Place the flat edge of the fitting on back of the cuff link.

Finishing off tie pins
Use hard solder to attach the pin to the main part of the piece.

Making a tie clip

1 Take a strip of metal about 60 x 5mm (2¼ x ¼in). Do not anneal the metal so that it retains its springiness. Place a former, such as the top end of a drill bit, in a vice. If you are using a drill bit, protect it by wrapping masking-tape around it before you place it in the vice. Use your fingers to bend the metal tightly around the former so that curve is a little less than halfway along its length.

3 Use half-round pliers to bend the second curve back towards the front again. Make another curve away again, using the former. It does not matter that the piece is too long at this stage.

4 Use flat-nosed pliers to pull the back past the front and to push it past the front to form a spring.

2 Bend a curve in the opposite direction around the same former.

5 Use a piercing saw to cut the back section to match the front.

Forging

Forging is a way of stretching, flattening, curving and shaping metal by applying force from different directions by means of specially shaped hammers, which are used from the top while the metal is supported on stakes of various shapes or on an anvil. Hammers and stakes used for forging should be kept highly polished so that no unnecessary marks are transferred to the metal. Clean the head of your hammer with fine wet and dry paper and then polish it with a mop or on some flat chamois leather before use.

Metal that has been forged has a wonderfully flowing quality, but if the process is to be successful you must use a piece of metal that is large enough to shape, curve, twist, file and finish, otherwise you will end up with a poorly proportioned, over-thin piece. It is easier to take metal away from a forged piece than it is to add it, although "simulated forging", which involves adding pieces of metal is also described here.

It is also easier to work to a drawn design. Lay the metal on top of the drawing while you work so that you can check that you have achieved the right curve and know where

the next one should start.

Forging stretches and compresses metal. For example, if you take a piece of metal measuring approximately 60 × 10mm (2¼ × ½in) and about 2mm (⅛in) thick and place it on a flat metal plate or anvil, you can lengthen it by hitting it with a rectangular raising or flat-faced hammer. Begin in the centre and bring the hammer, in even strokes, towards you, then, turn it around and repeat the process, so that each end is drawn out from the centre. If you want to spread the ends of the metal out more gradually, work in the same way but use a flat-faced hammer and increase the strength of the blows as you work along the metal.

The metal can be widened by working across the strip with a rectangular raising hammer, which is used along the line of the strip from one side to the other. If you work the same hammer down the centre of the strip, the edges will begin to curl upwards. If necessary they can be flattened again by annealing the strip and hitting it flat with a large flat-faced hammer.

SEE ALSO

- Annealing 14–15
- Filing 68–70
- Hammering 84–85

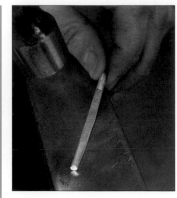

Forging
1 Use the flat head of a heavy hammer to broaden the end of a strip of metal. Work from the centre towards the area that is to be broadened.

2 Make sure that the area of metal being forged is in direct contact with the anvil or flat plate.

3 You can round square edges by gently working down the line with the ball end of a hammer.

4 Form a curve by hammering the outside edge only. Enlarging the outside edge in this way pushes the inside edge into a curve.

5 Reduce the hammer marks by using a planishing hammer.

6 Use a flat file to shape uneven edges.

7 An oval file can be used to neaten the inside curve.

Simulated forging

It is sometimes necessary to add an extra piece of metal to the side or top of a piece of forged metal. You may, for example, be forging a piece of 3mm (³⁄₁₆in) square wire and want to include a sweeping turn or bend. The wire is not sufficiently deep to create a flat area of 6mm (¹⁄₃in), and you will, therefore, need to solder a similar piece of 3mm (³⁄₁₆in) wire to the first length on the outside of the curve you intend to make. The bend is forged in the usual way then the metal is filed into shape.

1 Solder a strip of the same width to the area that is to be formed into a wide curve.

2 Forge the soldered piece in the same way as the single piece. When you are satisfied with the curve, remove the ends with your piercing saw and file the top and bottom surfaces to remove the solder join.

Sinusoidal stake – a curved stainless steel mandrel which is held on its straight length in the vice, used for anticlastic raising.

Anticlastic raising

This process of anticlastic raising adds an extra dimension to forging. The word "anticlastic" means that a piece has opposite curvatures at a given point – that is, it is curved convexly along a longitudinal plane and concavely along the perpendicular section.

The technique requires the use of a sinusoidal stake. The stake resembles a tapering, wavy line. Metal can be persuaded into a concave curve along its face while all the opposing curves, necessary to form a bangle, ring or necklace, can be formed at the same time. The stake can be made from steel, wood or plastic, as can the wedge-shaped hammer that is used to form the metal against it. Although a metal hammer used against a metal stake forms the work quickly, the piece may then need planishing to restore a smooth surface to the metal. It is preferable to use a wooden or a plastic hammer against a steel stake or vice versa. The forming may take a little longer, but it will need less finishing.

An annealed metal sheet is held squarely between the thumb and forefinger on the curve while the hammer, held in the other hand, is used to make small overlapping blows along the top edge of the metal, which is rotated slowly down over the stake. The hammer should strike the metal at 90 degrees and just below the point of contact between the metal and stake.

One continuous line is worked across the top edge before the piece is turned through 180 degrees so that the other edge can be worked in the same way. Working in this way stretches the outside areas of the metal and creates a concave curve, known as an axial curve, while the centre section of the metal is compressed and forced into a convex curve, which is called the generator curve.

Continue to make passes with the cross-pien hammer, working into the centre of the metal. Only when the whole piece has been worked will it be necessary to anneal the metal. The compression may cause a ridge to appear along the centre of the metal, but after annealing this can be carefully planished flat by another pass over the stake.

You can achieve different degrees of concave curves by working the metal over tighter curves of the stake. When all the concave curves have been made, the piece is placed against an ordinary ring mandrel to bring the somewhat oval shape that has formed into a circle or whatever shape is required. Maintain direct contact between the hammer, the metal and the mandrel and allow the piece to become hard and springy, which will give it its strength.

Anticlastic raising
Place a piece of silver on the sinusoidal stake in the centre of a curve and hold the ends between the finger and thumb of one hand. The silver strip must be laid directly over the curve before you begin – that is, there will be a gap between the silver and the stake. Hold the metal firmly all the time you are working.

2 After one or two passes on the first curve of the sinusoidal stake, make a tighter curve on one of the smaller curves of the stake, which can be turned around if necessary. Always hold both ends of the strip to keep the generator curve intact.

1 Use a cross-pien hammer to hit along the top edge of the metal. Work along the whole line, in a series of overlapping blows, then return to the beginning to work another line just below the first. Turn the silver through 180 degrees and work along the opposite edge in the same way. Continue to work in this way until the whole strip has passed along the stake.

4 Give the edges an extra-close curve by placing the strip on a flat plate and gently tapping it over with a light jeweller's hammer. Turn it over and tap down the other side.

3 The generator curve is defined on an ordinary mandrel. Try to keep the area of silver that is being worked in contact with the mandrel so that the work is as smooth as possible.

5 The strip after raising but before finishing, together with a ring worked in the same way.

Fusing

Metal can be joined without solder by simply heating it to the temperature at which it starts to melt. As the surface of the metal begins to move, any areas that are touching will fuse together.

Fusing can be a rather haphazard and unpredictable process, or it can be reasonably well controlled. In the first example shown here, the ring is made from pieces of scrap, and although the fusing process worked, it would be impossible to repeat the procedure to produce an identical piece. The second example is more controlled, and it would be possible to repeat the sequence and produce several similar pieces.

A piece of metal that is thin or a section of metal that stands away from the main area will probably melt before the rest of the piece has heated up adequately to fuse. If one piece of metal is too far away from another, one of them will melt first and become a rather amorphous mass before the other has had an opportunity to fuse to it. It is, however, possible to push and prod small bits of metal into place with a titanium soldering stick.

Quenching and rinsing

A fused join is as strong as a soldered join, but because the surface of the metal has started to melt and move, it will have a mottled appearance when it is cool. Also, the surface can be rather porous after fusing, which can cause problems when the metal is immersed in acid because the acid will tend to find its way into the metal. Unless properly neutralized, the acid will seep out and appear as an unattractive green blotch. To overcome this problem, drop the fused metal into hot water after heating and then place it in the acid or pickle bath. When the oxidization has disappeared, boil the piece in a solution of soda crystals and water, which will neutralize any remaining acid. You will still have to give the piece a thorough scrubbing either with pumice powder or with detergent after it has been neutralized, and if any joins are subsequently soldered, you will have to follow the same cleaning procedure.

Fusing wire

Thin wire, up to about 1.3mm (1/32in), can be laid on metal as it is fusing. It can be twirled in a fairly long piece or added in little bits as decoration.

Thin wire is easy to melt and to fuse, and it can be used in several ways. Hold a length of wire vertically with a pair of insulated tweezers so that one end dangles in front of a charcoal block. Concentrate the heat of the flame on a point just above the end of the wire and watch it carefully as it runs and forms a ball on the end of the wire.

Gold wire, which can be up to 0.75mm in diameter and in 14 or 18 carats, can be bent and twisted to form a ring or bangle and then joined by fusing. All the parts to be fused should be touching, and the ends of the wire can be left proud so that they will run up into little balls in direct heat. Concentrate the heat of the flame on the areas to be fused and watch the surface of the metal carefully until you can see that fusion has taken place.

Granulation

Small metal balls can also be soldered or fused onto jewellery as decoration.

To fuse silver balls to a silver base, you will find that they fuse more easily if there is a layer of copper between them. You can achieve this by pickling the balls in a solution of sulphuric acid and introducing a piece of steel or iron to the pickle. If steel is placed in pickle – as you may

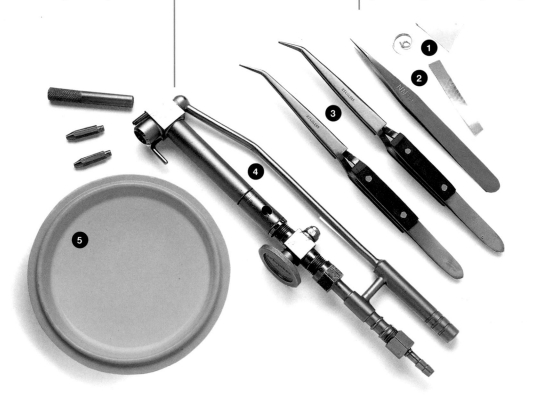

have seen if you have accidentally quenched a piece with binding wire still in place – a pinkish copper deposit will appear on the silver. Rinse the balls in water, dry them and place them with a little flux on the piece. Heat the metal until the balls just fuse to the surface.

To solder the balls to the metal, flux the base of each ball and place it in position. Hold a strip of easy solder over the balls and file the end with a needle file so that tiny solder filings fall all over and between the balls. Keep a stainless steel or a titanium stick in your hand as you solder so that you can reposition any balls that move.

SEE ALSO

- Annealing 14–15
- Doming & swaging 46–49
- Pickling & quenching 98–99

1 Scraps of silver sheet and wire for fusing together;
2 stainless steel tweezers;
3 insulated tweezers to hold pieces in position and for placing metal during fusing;
4 soldering torch – this is a hand-operated gas torch which has a small length of rubber hose pipe attached to the smaller terminal for the introduction of blown air. A further rubber hose for the gas is attached to the larger terminal; 5 liquid flux (Auflux), only small amounts are required and the liquid should always be returned to its container after use.

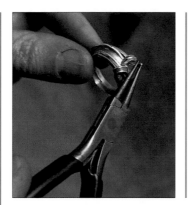

2 Cover the silver with flux, place it on a soldering block and heat it.

3 When the surface begins to move, hold the flame steady to keep the temperature constant. Allow the scrap pieces to mould to each other. This is the crucial time – if you apply too much heat the silver simply becomes a mess, and if there is insufficient heat the piece will not fuse. Take it to the point at which you think that the piece will work as a ring.

Making a ring from scrap
1 Bend scrap pieces of silver into the approximate shape of a ring.

4 Rinse, pickle, rinse and clean the ring, then use a piercing saw to cut away any unwanted areas. If you wish, use a file to model it further.

5 Polish the ring or simply burnish the highlights.

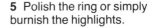

Making a fused wire ring
1 Take two pieces of D-section wire or round wire, approximately 2mm (1/16in) in diameter, that are exactly the same length and form them into rings.

2 Fuse the join together on both rings, place them on a mandrel and then hammer them until they are round.

3 Place one ring on top of the other and flux the centre, where they meet. Fuse the two together.

4 Use dividers to mark the section you want to remove.

5 Cut it out with a piercing saw.

6 Bend the ring so that the ends meet and place the cut-out section over the join.

7 Flux the joins.

8 Fuse the ring together, this time keeping a careful watch on the amount of heat you apply so that the ring fuses but does not melt.

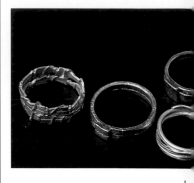

9 Four silver rings, made by fusing.

Fusing gold and silver
1 Paint some flux onto the cut-out gold pattern and place it, flux side down, in the centre of the silver.

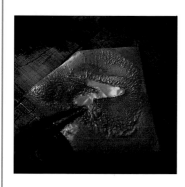

2 Heat the silver until the surface starts to move and press the gold down onto it, using a titanium soldering stick or tweezers.

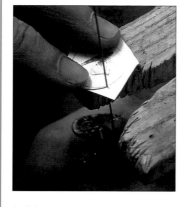

3 After pickling, boil the earrings in a solution of soda crystals to neutralize the acid. Use a piercing saw to cut out the silver circle and then rinse thoroughly.

4 Dome the circle (see Doming and Swaging, pages 46–49) and solder the earring fitting to the back.

Making balls for granulation
1 Make a small indentation in the charcoal block and place a little piece of wire, 2–3mm (about ⅛in) long, in it. Heat it up.

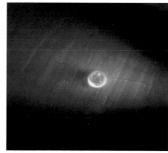

2 Watch the metal until it starts to shine and forms a spinning ball. Remove the flame and, when it has cooled slightly, pickle the ball until it is shiny.

3 The balls can be soldered or fused to the work.

Hammering

The array of different hammers used in jewellery and silversmithing can be rather overwhelming at first, and it is difficult to select the one or two that will be useful and versatile. Hammers have different heads for different purposes: a round, flat-faced head on one end with a round domed or wedge-shaped at the other is the kind of hammer with which most of us are familiar, but there are also rounded rectangular heads, broad, flat heads, wedge-shaped heads, square block heads, round heads and many more, all made for specific purposes.

One factor that must be considered is the weight of the hammer. A light hammer is used for riveting or hitting a chasing tool, for example. A heavy hammer used for these tasks would be unbalanced and difficult to use evenly.

It is important that metal is kept well annealed during all the stages of hammering, except when it is being made springy. If the metal becomes too hard when it is being hammered it will crack.

Other hammers

A **planishing hammer** – that is, one with a flat, highly polished face – is used to smooth out marks made by other hammers. The planishing hammer is worked in the same direction as the ordinary hammer.

A planishing hammer or the polished, flat head of a **ballpien (ballpeen) hammer** is used to stretch, strengthen and add springiness to rings, bangles, neckpieces, pins and so on. If a length of wire that is going to be used for a neckpiece needs to be springy, for example, the wire is first annealed and then the whole length is coiled around a section of the mandrel that is a few sizes smaller than the required finished size. It is then hammered around the mandrel as it is gradually pushed down to increase the diameter. By the time the wire has reached the full diameter, it will be springy.

Mallets are either wooden or are made from rawhide or rubber. They are used to shape metal against a metal stake, but because they are relatively soft they do not mark it. Used on its own, a mallet will not stretch metal nor harden it to any great degree.

Using hammers

When you use a hammer, the head should always make positive contact with the metal. Use it at an angle so that the face meets the metal squarely and does not leave edge marks. This is just as important for the metal stake on which a piece of metal is supported. Any damage caused by a hammer on a stake will mark the underside of any new piece of metal that is used with that stake. Badly damaged stakes can be professionally reground, and hammers used only for shaping metal should be kept polished and dry.

The action of the hammer comes from the wrist. The weight of head is balanced against the weight of the handle, so that a rhythmic movement can develop, which makes it possible to hit the metal with blows of equal pressure. Hammer marks left during the making process have to be removed so that the piece has a smooth, shiny finish. The more even the marks are, the more easily they can be removed or smoothed out with a planishing hammer.

SEE ALSO

- Annealing 14–15
- Chasing & repoussé 42–45
- Engraving 60–63

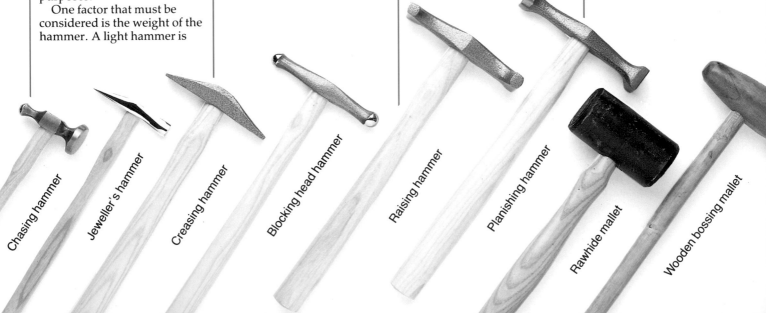

Chasing hammer

Jeweller's hammer

Creasing hammer

Blocking head hammer

Raising hammer

Planishing hammer

Rawhide mallet

Wooden bossing mallet

Holding and using hammers
A **wooden mallet** or a **rawhide mallet** is used to round a ring on a mandrel.

Use a polished hammer head for planishing a surface or enlarging a ring. This can be either a **planishing hammer** or the clean head of an ordinary hammer.

A **creasing hammer** is used to curve metal in a swaging block. The hammer hits the centre line of the metal, and this forces it up into a curve.

You can use a **ball head** or a **blocking head** to produce a curved or a rounded effect.

Use a little **jeweller's hammer** to harden pins, tap down rivets and so on. Harden pins by rolling them along a flat plate or the top of an anvil, tapping along the metal with the hammer as you do so.

A **blocking hammer** gives a gentle curve to a copper dish. Turn the dish in the wooden block and tap rhythmically, working outwards from the centre or from the point at which the curve begins.

Use the flat face of an **ordinary hammer** for hitting the head of a doming punch or a punch that you have made yourself with a diameter of 15mm (⅝in).

The underside of the bowl can be planished with a **planishing hammer**. Place the piece on a metal stake that reflects the curve you have made and work gently around the piece with the hammer to smooth out the hammer marks made earlier.

A **chasing hammer**, which is balanced for light, continuous hammering, can be used to curve over the edges when you make chenier.

Inlaying

1 Brass sheet with contrasting silver wire; **2** chisel type gravers with different-sized cutting edges; **3** large punch for tapping wire into grooves; **4** wooden handles for graver chisels.

Fine metal lines can be laid into contrasting metals or into other media, such as wood, to produce intricate patterns and designs in a finely finished surface. The traditional method is for the inlaid metal to be held in channels or grooves that are chiselled from the background metal. The grooves are cut in such a way that a burr is raised on either side of the cut; these burrs are pushed down and burnished over the fine metal wire that is laid in the channels.

There are some remarkable examples of extraordinarily detailed Japanese metal inlay work, and it is worth looking in your local museum to see some of the finest work of this kind from around the world.

The technique illustrated here will enable you to achieve the same effect without having to master completely the skills of accurate chisel and tool work that are essential for traditional inlay work. It is, however, important to understand the principles underlying traditional method by which fine wire is laid into the surface of another metal.

The metal
Use a metal that contrasts well with the wire that is to be inlaid. The metal should be 1– 2mm (1/32in) thick, so that a sufficiently deep channel to accommodate the wire can be cut without a mark appearing on the back when the wire is hammered in. The thinner the metal you use, the finer should be the wire that is inlaid.

The metal should be annealed and then held flat in firm pitch or in jeweller's wax. The lines for inlay should be transferred directly onto the metal by tracing through the design, or by marking the metal with a pencil or scriber.

The wire
You can use either round or rectangular wire. It should be well annealed and fit closely into the channel. Fine silver and gold wires, which are soft and flexible, are ideal for inlay work, but whatever you use must be a strong contrast with the background metal.

The tools
A **chasing hammer** is used to hit the top of the **chisel** as it cuts into the metal. The chisel is held at the same angle as a tracing punch – that is, it is held between the thumb and first finger of one hand with the handle pointing away from your body while your other fingers rest on the metal. The chisel is worked towards you along the prepared line.

The cut, which is the essence of inlay, must be undercut. This means that the edges are raised slightly during cutting so that when the wire is laid in position, the edges are hammered down and so hold the wire in position.

The chisel has a cutting

edge, of which the bottom edge is somewhat ground away to enable a very fine line to be cut. Chisels used for cutting metal do not have wooden handles, like those used for working with wood. The handles are made of steel stock, and the cutting end should be tempered.

A **matting or embossing punch** is used to beat the wire into the channel. It is held vertically above the wire and hammered with a chasing hammer or a heavier hammer if necessary. The face of the punch must be wide enough to spread across both the inlaid wire and the raised edges of the channel.

The groove or channel can also be cut with **engraving tools**. The first line is cut with a graver with a lozenge-shaped head, and the base of this line is broadened by a flat-edged graver. Wire can be punched into the groove, but it will need to be held in place with solder because there is no raised edge to push down to hold the wire in place. Use the smallest possible amount of solder and file the surface level after soldering.

Inlaying the wire
Place one end of the wire at the start of the chiselled groove and tap it into place with a punch to make sure that it is held firmly. The wire is then inserted gradually into the line, pressed into place by the punch as you work along the channel. The main object of the process is to push over the edges of the groove that were raised during chiselling. When the wire has been pushed into place, a burnisher can be used to smooth the top of the wire

and any rough edges.

If you are using a rectangular wire for the inlay, burnish along the bottom edge to create a slight overhang that will fit snugly into the chiselled groove.

SEE ALSO

- Annealing 14–15
- Using wire 128–133

1 Draw the pattern to be inlaid on the surface of the silver.

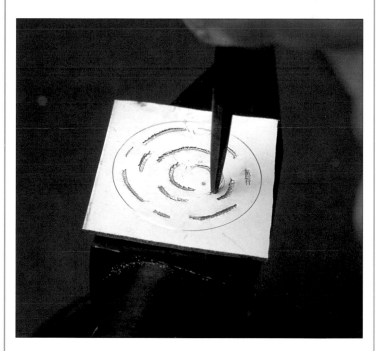

2 Use a punch that is no wider than the wire that is to be inlaid and, holding the punch above the work, strike it with a medium weight hammer. Work smoothly along the lines of the design, overlapping each stroke as you make the next one.

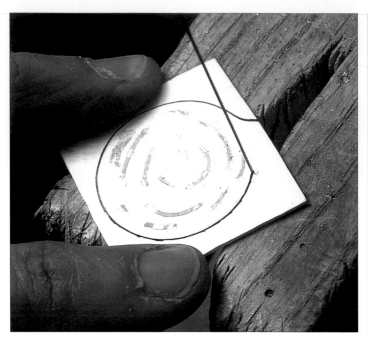

3 Cut the wire into appropriate lengths and bend each piece to fit the line made by the punch. Lay all the pieces in position, making sure that none of the wires is longer than the punched groove and that no wire protrudes over the edges of the groove in which it is positioned.

4 Place the piece on a flat plate and place another flat plate over it. Strike the plate with a heavy hammer, held upright over the plate.

5 Flux all around the flattened wires and place a paillon of solder at each end of each wire. Solder them in place. Pierce around the shape. This piece was then domed (see Doming and Swaging, pages 46–49) and further soldering was completed with medium and easy solder.

6 Use a coarse file to remove the sections of wire protruding above the surface of the metal. Then use a finer file before working through the grades of wet and dry papers until the surface of the metal is absolutely smooth and the two metals look as one.

Inlaying larger pieces of metal
When you are inlaying larger areas of metal into each other, the piece being inlaid should fit exactly into the receiving metal. If you cut the shape to receive the inlay first, use the cut-out piece as a template around which you can scribe the shape onto the inlay metal. The shape should be fractionally larger than the template to allow for the width of the saw blade in the receiving metal. File the inlay piece so that it fits exactly.

1 Draw accurately the area to be removed from the main piece of metal.

2 Drill a fine hole just in from the scribed line, thread the saw blade through the hole and pierce out the shape. The piercing must be done as precisely as possible because the success of the technique lies in accurate cutting.

3 Place the cut-out pattern onto the metal that is to be used for the inlay. Hold it steady and scribe around the outside. Pierce around the line and use a file to smooth the shape until it fits exactly into the cut-out shape.

4 Press the cut-out shape into the metal and paint flux in the area to be jointed. Turn the piece over so that solder can be applied to the back of the piece. Solder it in place.

5 A circle was scribed around the star and the shape cut out and domed before being polished.

Mokumé Gané

This technique is used to decorate the surface of metal by producing a fine decoration that resembles the grain of wood. It is a traditional Japanese technique, which is used both to create decorative patterns and to give a detailed background on exceptionally fine Japanese metalwork.

The effect is achieved by sandwiching together several metals and then exposing the different colours of the metals on the surface. Up to five sheets of coloured metal can be soldered together, and you can use combinations of nickel, silver, copper, brass, monel metal, standard silver, fine silver and white, red or yellow gold. The metal sheets should be a similar thickness, approximately 0.5mm, although, because of its cost, the gold can be thinner. The gold will appear only as a fine line in the pattern if the original sheet is extremely thin.

After the sheets are soldered together, they are put through a rolling mill and reduced to a thickness of about 1mm (1/32in). The metals will need to be annealed during this process. The sheet is then cut into two equal pieces, and one half is placed on top of the other, with the two pieces being soldered together as before. This process of cutting and soldering can be repeated as often as you wish because the number of layers is doubled each time.

After the last soldering to join one half to the other, the piece of metal can be pickled and then rinsed thoroughly and dried. It is then either worked from the back or indentations are made from the front to create a random or regular pattern. A variety of tools can be used on the front, including different burrs on a pendant motor, chisels and tracer punches, and they can be used to different depths in the metal.

The metal is then passed through the rolling mill until it is completely flat. After this, the sheet is annealed, and at this stage it can be pickled, although ideally it should be boiled out in a solution of soda crystals and water and rinsed.

Using mokumé gané
The piece of mokumé gané is then ready to be used. You may decide to solder it into or onto another metal, when you should use easy solder, or you could set it into another metal and rivet it. It can be polished in the usual way. To add to the effects of the colour, you could, depending on the mixture of metals used, allow the standard silver to oxidize after polishing by applying gentle heat and allowing the piece to cool in the air.

SEE ALSO

- Annealing 14–15
- Polishing 104–105
- Soldering 112–115
- Texturing 126–127

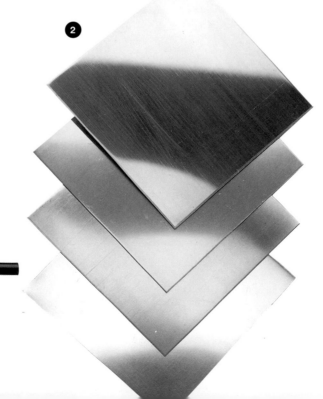

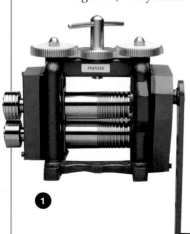

1 Rolling mill for compressing sheets of soldered metals;
2 sheets of silver, copper and brass to be soldered together.

Assembling the layers

1 Carefully clean all the pieces of metal that are to be used. Remove all traces of grease by holding each piece under running water and rubbing it with wet and dry paper until the water stays all over the surface of the metal and does not form individual globules.

3 Cut a stick of hard or medium solder, flux it and then run it over the surface of the metal.

4 Use a titanium spreader to make sure that the solder covers the whole surface of the metal. Maintain a constant heat for this.

2 Paint one side of one of the pieces with borax or flux.

5 Repeat steps 1–4 on one side of the second piece of metal, then clean the metal with pumice powder paste and rinse well, but do not quench it in acid.

6 Place the first piece, soldered side up, on a charcoal block. Paint the unsoldered side of the second piece with flux and place it, flux side down, on top of the first piece. Paint one side of the third piece with flux and place it, flux side down, on the second sheet. Heat the three sheets all the way through to bring them all to soldering temperature and watch the solder flow, adding more solder from a stick if necessary.

8 Pass the metal sandwich through a rolling mill.

7 Remove the flame. Place a piece of flat, heavy metal on the surface of the metal sandwich and leave it for a few minutes. Rinse and dry the metal.

9 When the sandwich begins to become hard, place it on the charcoal block and anneal. Cut the piece in half with a piercing saw.

10 Paint the underside of one side with flux and place it over the other half. Solder the two pieces together.

11 Cut in half, reflux and resolder again as many times as you want to build up the individual layers.

12 Use the flat plate again to press the mokumé gané sandwich together after soldering.

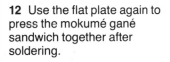

13 Some solder will be squeezed out around the edges by the weight of the flat plate, but this is not a problem.

14 Pass the metal through the mill until it is half the thickness and repeat from step 9 if you wish.

Making the pattern
1 Place the piece in pitch or on a sandbag and make indentations in the back of the metal with doming punches or with different shaped metal punches.

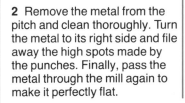

2 Remove the metal from the pitch and clean thoroughly. Turn the metal to its right side and file away the high spots made by the punches. Finally, pass the metal through the mill again to make it perfectly flat.

Patinating and Oxidizing

The process of patination is associated with copper, bronze and, sometimes, brass. It is a film formed on the surface of the metal, either through natural exposure to the air or by treatment with acids or chemicals, which alters the colour of the metals.

Oxidization occurs when metal is exposed to air and damp, allowing the sulphur content that is present in the atmosphere to discolour and blacken the metal. Oxidization also occurs when an oxidizing flame is used to heat metal. The heat from the flame combines with the oxygen in the air and forms a film of oxide on the surface of the metal. The process can be simulated chemically by placing metal into "liver of sulphur" or a potassium sulphide solution. The chemicals in the sulphur solution combine with the metal to form a coloured surface.

If liver of sulphur is used in a hot solution, standard silver and golds that are less than 18 carat will turn black. A few drops of household ammonia can be added to give an even deeper black. If the solution is warm, rather than hot, the colours will range from yellow-grey, through to some wonderful shades of blue, pink and purple. These colours are not, however, stable unless a coat of lacquer or beeswax is applied. When it is used cold, liver of sulphur will colour copper but will have little or an unpleasant effect on silver.

Metal that is to be patinated or oxidized should be completely clean – all residues of flux must be removed, for example – and if it has been polished all traces of polish must be removed together with any fingermarks.

The piece is suspended in an oxidizing solution by means of a copper wire. The solution is most effective when it is deep yellow in colour and, if it is being used hot, it should not be boiling. Mix only the amount you will need for one application because the solution quickly spoils. The solution can also be painted onto specific areas with a fine paintbrush, and you will find it easier to work if the metal is warmed slightly before you begin.

Colouring Recipes

- Silver and gold to black:
1cm sq (½in sq) potassium sulphide
300–600ml (½–1 pint) water few drops ammonia
- Silver and gold to dark grey (the gold should be warm when it is being dipped):
1cm sq (½in sq) potassium sulphide
300–600ml (½–1 pint) water
- Copper and brass to black:
Hot solution of ammonium sulphide
- Copper and brass to green (the solution is used hot and painted on the metal):
1.5g copper nitrate
200ml (6fl oz) water
- Copper and brass to dark green (mix a paste and apply; leave to dry before washing off and exposing the metal to sunlight):
1 part copper sulphate
1 part zinc chloride
1 part water

When you have achieved the colour you want, rinse the piece thoroughly because any solution that is left on the metal will continue to work.

If you need to remove the colour, you can scratch or brush it off, or you can heat the object and pickle it, or you can simply polish it. Other colouring effects can be achieved by the use of chemicals.

SEE ALSO

- Annealing 14–15
- Polishing 104–105

1 Potassium sulphide (liver of sulphur);
2 liver of sulphur;
3 patinating mix of sawdust, ammonia and vinegar.

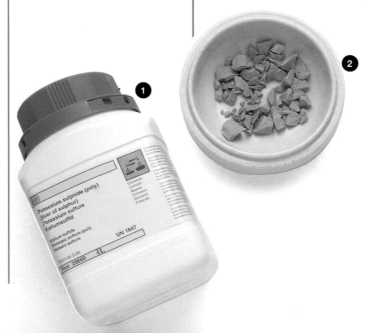

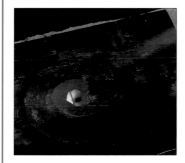

Making a pair of patinated copper earrings

1 Cut a piece of copper to the desired shape and hammer it, using either a planishing hammer or the ball end of a ball-pien hammer to give the surface a good texture. Clean both the front and back of the piece with pumice paste, rinse and dry. Coat the front surface with borax paste.

2 Use your torch to heat the front surface of the metal.

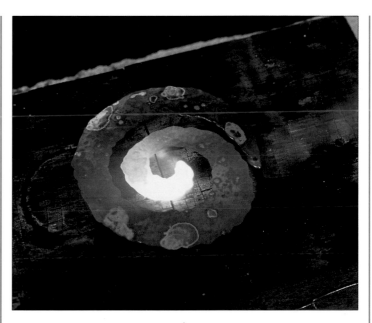

4 Turn over the piece and heat it again until it glows. Wait about 1 minute, then quench the piece in cold water. The black firescale will flake off and the colour will start to appear. Clean the piece by immersing it for about 3 minutes in a sulphuric acid solution to remove any traces of borax.

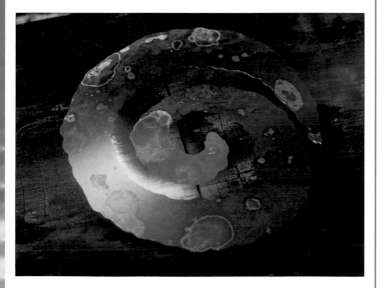

3 Continue to heat the metal until it begins to glow a deep reddish-orange. Immediately remove the torch.

5 Leave the pieces matt and seal them with a layer of beeswax. The red oxidization is permanent.

Giving brass a green patina
1 For each earring you will need two domes, each of a different size.

2 Solder a spiral wire onto the domes. Clean the surface thoroughly with wet and dry papers to remove all traces of fire stain.

3 Make a solution of 4 parts household liquid ammonia and 1 part vinegar and mix it with either fine, clean, wet sawdust or rolling tobacco. Use an old plastic tub or carton that held margarine or ice-cream and that has a fairly tight-fitting lid. Bury the earrings in the mixture and replace the lid on the carton.

4 Leave the brass pieces in the mixture for up to 24 hours, then remove them and leave them to air-dry. Use a toothbrush to remove the bits of sawdust or tobacco that adhere to the surface.

5 Rub the surface of the decoration with wet and dry papers.

6 Seal with beeswax or a coat of transparent lacquer.

Patinating copper
Copper can be treated in the same way as brass.

Oxidizing silver

1 Make sure the piece to be treated is completely finished, then put about 1cm sq (½in sq) of potassium sulphate into 300–600ml (½–1 pint) boiling water. Allow the potassium to dissolve – the smell will be unpleasant. Attach a piece of silver or copper wire to the piece to be oxidized and lower it into the solution. Wait until it is completely black before removing it. If the mixture is not hot enough it will take longer or possibly not even turn black at all but a blue-purple colour. Although attractive, the blue-purple is not stable and will probably darken with time.

2 Highlights can be created by polishing off the oxidization with a burnisher or a mop. Be careful not to remove more than you want.

Pickling and Quenching

Pickling is the word used to describe chemically cleaning a piece of metal after it has been heated. Quenching describes the cooling of metal after heating. Both processes can be carried out in a variety of ways.

Pickling
While they are heated brass, copper, nickel silver, silver and golds up to and including 18 carat will oxidize to different degrees. The oxidization appears on the surface of the metal as a greyish-black film, which is removed chemically in an acid solution. Oxides can also be removed with wet and dry papers, fine files and so on, but this also removes minute amounts of metal, and chemical methods are, therefore, preferred.

Dirty or greasy metal must be annealed and then pickled in an acid solution to clean it before soldering can take place. After soldering, use pickle to remove any residual flux because if it is not removed straightaway, the flux becomes crusty and is awkward to remove by hand.

Quenching
Metal can be quenched either in water or in a pickling solution. You should quench in water if you are using either an alum or a hot pickle solution.

After annealing or soldering allow the metal to cool slightly before quenching. If you do not, you may cause stresses within the structure of the metal that will distort it and the pickling solution will spit violently and give off fumes.

Leave copper and silver for a few seconds, then use a pair of brass tweezers to place the hot metal in the pickling solution. Remove any binding wire that was used to hold pieces together for soldering. If you place binding wire or steel or iron tweezers in a pickling solution containing sulphuric acid you will contaminate the solution and everything that is subsequently placed in it.

Before quenching gold, check the technical

Safety Procedures

Most pickling solutions contain acid, and they are, therefore, potentially dangerous. When you are mixing a pickle, take a few obvious precautions:

- Make sure that you have easy access to running water in case of spills.
- Always store bottles containing acid where they cannot accidentally be knocked over and, ideally, in a lockable cupboard. Make sure that all bottles are clearly labelled.
- Wear rubber gloves, eye protectors and, preferably, a heavy-duty apron or overall.
- Work in a well-ventilated room or even outdoors because acids give off pungent fumes.
- Always add acid to water; never add water to neat acid.

specifications that will have been supplied with the metal when you obtained it from the dealer. Some golds do not require quenching at all, and others must be quenched below specific temperatures.

Preparing and using pickling solutions
If you spill sulphuric acid, even when it is diluted, onto clothing, a hole will appear after the next washing. There is nothing you can do about this, which is why you should wear a thick apron or, at the very least, old clothes. If you get any sulphuric acid on your skin, rinse it under clear running water; it will leave your skin feeling sore and inflamed. Nitric acid solution splashes on your skin will cause black stains and make your skin feel itchy. Again, rinse the affected area under clear running water.

A suitable solution for pickling silver, gold or copper can be made from 1 part sulphuric acid to 10 parts water.

For pickling gold, use a solution of 1 part nitric acid to 8 parts water. Keep this separate and use it only for gold, because if you clean gold in a solution that has been used mainly for silver, a silver deposit may be left on the surface of the gold.

Sulphuric acid solution can be used hot or cold. Mix it in an ovenproof glass bowl or jug with a lid to prevent evaporation. If you are using a warm pickle, place the bowl containing the solution in a second bowl of warm water, which is then heated. Do not place sulphuric acid in a pan or bowl that is subjected to direct heat.

It is possible to obtain special hot pickle tanks made of reinforced plastic. The outer casing containing the water has a thermostatically controlled heater, while the acid solution is held in an inner section.

Alum pickle
Alum is most often used as an astringent or paper mordant, but it can be used to clean and pickle metal. It acts more slowly than an acid solution but is safer for use in the home workshop. Make a solution of 50g (1½oz) in 0.5 litre (1 pint) of warm water. Mix it either in a fireproof bowl or jug with a cover so that it can be kept warm over a gentle heat or in a ceramic slow cooker.

Quench heated work in cold water, then place it in the warm alum and leave it until clean.

Proprietary pickling solutions
Your tool and equipment supplier will stock a proprietary, ready-made pickling solution. Read the manufacturer's instructions carefully before use.

"Spent" pickle
After it has been used several times, pickle becomes "spent" – that is, inactive. This will be obvious as the colour turns deeper and deeper blue and the pickle takes longer and longer to work.

When you dispose of spent pickle, turn on the cold tap and let it run for a while before slowly pouring away the pickle. Leave the tap running while you do this and for a short time afterwards. **Never pour away fresh acid in this way.**

3 Mix 50g (1½oz) alum with 0.5 litre (1 pint) water. You can buy alum in most chemists shops.

Preparing pickles
1 Wear thick rubber gloves when you prepare a pickle that contains acid and always add the acid to water – not the other way around.

2 If you leave binding wire on a piece of silver that is being pickled, the metal will turn red when the iron in the wire reacts with the acid. Anything subsequently pickled in the solution will be contaminated.

2 Placing a piece of hot silver in a sulphuric acid solution (10 parts water to 1 part acid) will remove any black oxides.

Using pickles
1 When it is used warm, alum will remove oxides and flux residues as effectively as sulphuric acid. Use an ovenproof bowl or jug with a lid.

3 After being quenched in cold water, pieces can be placed in a hot pickle tank to remove the oxides.

4 Make a solution of soda crystals dissolved in hot water. If you are not sure that all the acid has been rinsed away, submerge the piece in the solution of soda crystals and boil it for a minute or two.

Piercing

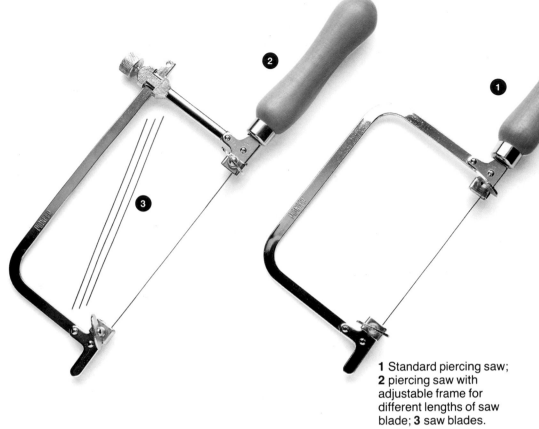

1 Standard piercing saw;
2 piercing saw with
adjustable frame for
different lengths of saw
blade; 3 saw blades.

The **piercing saw** is one of the most essential tools in a jeweller's workshop. At first, however, working with a piercing saw can be rather frustrating because the blades used are small and they can break easily. Sometimes a single blade will last for weeks, sometimes you will get through an entire packet in an afternoon. Don't worry – it happens to everyone.

Blade sizes range from 4, through 0 to 06, which is the finest and is used with metal that is as thin as 0.3–0.4mm. Use a no. 4 blade for cutting metal that is 2–3mm (1/16in) thick, or for cutting acrylic up to 5–6mm (about 1/4in) thick.

Begin by practising on a piece of metal about 1mm (1/32in) thick and with a size no. 1 or 01 blade.

A **coping saw** is about one and a half times larger than a piercing saw, but it is used in the same way. A **fretsaw** is useful for cutting from a large sheet of metal as it enables you to cut your pattern without having to cut away small pieces or cut from many different angles.

Fixing a blade
Sit so that you can hold the handle of the saw in one hand and the blade in the other and so that you can push the head of the saw against something solid, such as the side of your work bench.

Hold the blade with the teeth facing towards you but pointing down, towards the handle of the saw. Run your fingers down the blade. If it feels smooth, the blade is correctly positioned; if it does not, turn it the other way up. Place the top end of the blade into the top fixing point of the saw and tighten it. Push the handle of the saw against the bench and fasten the lower end of the saw into the bottom fixing. The blade should be taut before you start work.

Holding the saw
Hold the handle of the saw as lightly as possible and let the saw do the work. The cut is made on the down stroke, so try to develop a rhythm whereby the saw almost falls through the work and needs only a gentle hand to guide it up again. Keep it upright, so that the blade is at an angle of 90 degrees to your work unless you are deliberately cutting an angle.

Using the saw
Hold the saw upright, with the blade just touching the line on the metal you wish to cut. Place the index finger of your other hand against the side of the saw and use it as a guide as you move the saw up and down and gently forwards into the metal.

When you begin to use the piercing saw, you may find it helpful to cut between two close parallel lines. For example, when you are cutting a strip of metal to make a ring, set a pair of dividers to the required width, place one side of the dividers on the straight edge of the metal and use the other side of the dividers to draw a line parallel to it. Open out the dividers by a further millimetre or so, and draw a second line, parallel to the first. Pierce between the two lines.

You may also find it helpful to cut circles in this way at first. Use dividers to scribe the circle on the metal, open them a further millimetre and scribe a second circle. Cut between the lines and use a file to neaten the edge down to the first scribed line.

Turning corners
Cut to the edge of a corner and, while you keep the saw moving in rhythm, use the smooth back edge to work around the corner. Pretend to be cutting backwards and, once the corner is turned, continue with the forward movement.

Piercing out central areas
If the pattern has enclosed areas, use a small drill to make a hole in the corner of each area. Unfasten the bottom end of the blade, thread it through a hole and refasten the blade tightly. Pierce out the area, undo the bottom end of the blade and thread it through the next area to be removed.

Using a piercing saw
1 Push the saw against the pin or against the side of the work bench and tighten the blade until it is firm and springy. A loose blade will be difficult to use and will break easily.

2 To make the first cut use your finger as a guide at the side of the blade and move the saw gently up and down until it has a purchase on the metal.

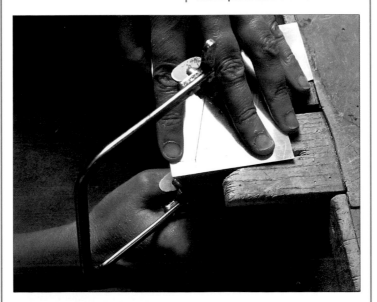

3 Turn a corner by pushing the back edge of the blade against the outside edge of the metal.

Move forwards again only when the turn is complete.

4 If the blade gets stuck, lift the saw and metal away from the pin and allow the metal to find its own balance by simply holding the saw and letting go of the metal. Carefully replace the metal in that position on the pin and the blade should be free to start cutting again.

Working large pieces

1 An extra large piercing saw is useful if you need to cut out one shape from a large piece of metal. Use it in exactly the same way as an ordinary piercing saw.

2 Using a coping saw for large items. Here a block of model-making wax is being cut to size. A coping saw can be used to cut wood – oak, for example.

Piercing central areas

When you need to cut areas from the centre of a piece of metal, drill a small hole and thread the bottom of the saw

blade through the hole. Refasten it tightly and cut out the required area. Clean inside edges with a fine saw blade (size 04/02), working with a gentle stroking action down the edge of the metal.

Cutting out a design

1 Draw the design on tracing paper, then coat the back of the tracing with a spray adhesive and place it on the metal.

2 Beginning in the centre, drill a hole in the areas to be cut out. Pierce along the lines of the tracing.

3 Complete all the piercing of the inside of the design before cutting out the outside shape. Peel off the tracing paper. If some paper is left, it will be burnt off during annealing.

Piercing a complex design

1 Draw the pattern on a piece of tracing paper. Rub the surface of the metal with Plasticine or putty and stick the tracing onto the metal.

2 Transfer the pattern to the surface of the metal and cut out the edges with a piercing saw. Remove the tracing paper and use a scriber to outline the traced lines of the pattern.

3 Solder together the ends of the ring and shape it on a triblet.

4 Draw a line around the centre of the ring and use the piercing saw to cut the ring into two halves.

5 Neaten the sawn edges with a flat file.

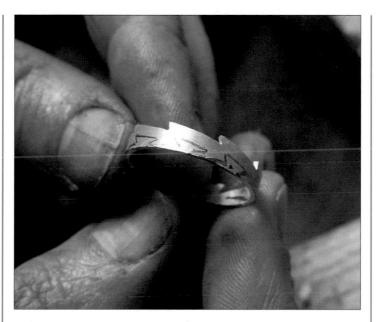

6 Go over the scribed lines of the pattern with a sharp pencil to make the lines easier to follow with the piercing saw.

7 Carefully pierce out the pattern from both sides.

8 Place the two halves of the ring back together and use easy solder to join them together. Clean and polish.

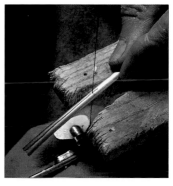

Cutting wire and chenier using a piercing saw

1 Mark the centre line with a pair of dividers, set to half the width of the metal. Place one side of the dividers against the edge of the wire and draw a line down the centre.

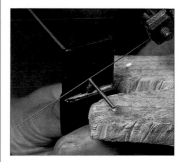

2 Use a jointing tool to hold chenier or wire if you want to cut a straight edge. Place the chenier through the tool until it is the right length and fasten the little screw to hold the chenier in place. Lean the blade of the saw against the edge of the tool to cut straight down through the chenier.

Polishing

Polishing gives metal a reflective shine and a smooth finish, and it is achieved either by systematic hand finishing or by the use of an electric motor with polishing mops.

Hand polishing

When you have finished a piece as far as fine grade wet and dry papers, you have several options. If you want a textured finish, turn to Texturing, pages 126–127. Here we discuss the ways in which you can give a piece a highly polished finish.

You can buy, or make, a **felt polishing stick**. This is a piece of wood, approximately 200 x 20 x 5mm (10 x 1 x ¼in), with a piece of thick felt, measuring 130 x 20mm (about 5 x 1in), stuck to one end. Squeeze some lighter fuel onto the felt and rub some **tripoli polish compound** into the fuel. Tripoli is a dark brown, fairly greasy polish, which is supplied in long blocks. Rub the felt briskly over the work. You will need two or three felt sticks, with a different polish on each one.

Spread a soft **chamois leather** over a flat surface, squeeze some lighter fuel on it and rub in some **fine rouge polish**, in either block or powder form. You can also use paraffin to dissolve rouge powder on the leather. Rub the work vigorously on the leather before cleaning off the polish with a clean cloth.

The inside of awkward areas can be polished with a shank of **fine strings**. Hang the shank over a hook or fasten them into a vice, and take as many of the strings as you will need. Soak these strings with lighter fuel and rub polish into the moist area. Thread the strings through the section that you want to polish and rub the piece holding the strings tight.

Liquid metal cleaners, which can also be used for plastics and acrylics, can be applied with a soft cotton cloth. Take care that you do not use a liquid that is too abrasive. Use an impregnated silver cloth to give a final shine to a piece, but these cloths alone will not polish metal.

Using a pendant motor

A pendant motor with a small mop attachment is ideal for polishing small or difficult areas. Polishing is a dirty and dusty job, and when you are working at your bench with a pendant motor, you can prevent the polish from flying everywhere by dipping the mop in paraffin before you apply the polish. As with hand-held polishing sticks, keep separate mops for each polish. Hold your work firmly in one hand, using the bench pin for support, and hold the shaft of the pendant motor in the other hand.

Using a polishing motor

A polishing motor has one or two arms to which different mops can be attached. You should try to make sure that the motor sits in some kind of box, with sufficient clear area around it for the spindle arm, in which all the polishing dust can be caught. Keep separate mops for the different kinds of polish.

When you use a polishing motor, always wear safety glasses, tie back any loose or long hair and do not wear any loose clothing or jewellery that might get caught in the revolving wheel. Screw the appropriate mop to the spindle and stand in line with your work so that you can see clearly what you are doing. Switch on the machine, then hold the polish against the mop for 2–3 seconds before holding your work firmly and squarely against the mop. Turn the work between polishing strokes, but remember that the mop has a very fast action, and it is easy to lose the crisp edges and corners by over-polishing. Place the sides of the piece directly on the mop, and any difficult angles can be worked by using the edge of the mop.

After the first polish with tripoli compound, clean and

1 Polishing motor with built in extractor;
2 lambswool mop on machine for rouge polish;
3 felt cone for polishing inside a ring; **4** felt lap;
5 calico mop; **6** abrasive mops.

dry the work before using another polish on another mop. At this point you can go straight to a soft calico or lambswool mop, used with a rouge polish.

Cleaning
When you have polished the articles, clean them by placing them in an ovenproof dish of hot water and either a liquid cleaning agent or a domestic detergent to which you have added a teaspoon of ammonia.

SEE ALSO
- Basic tools 8–9

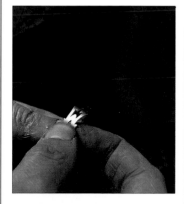

Polishing a ring on a polishing motor
1 Hold a ring in both hands so that it is just below the horizontal axis of the mop. (If you imagine that the vertical axis runs from 12 o'clock to 6 o'clock and the horizontal axis runs from 9 o'clock to 3 o'clock, you should hold the work at about 4 o'clock.)

2 Polish the inside of a ring on a felt cone, which should be screwed to the shaft of the polishing motor. Hold the ring with both hands and press the sides against the cone while you rotate the ring.

Polishing a chain on a polishing motor
1 When you are polishing a chain, wrap it around the handle of an emery stick so that there are no loops that might get caught up in the mop. Hold each section against the polishing mop, moving the chain around the stick, section by section.

2 If you want to polish a chain without a stick, hold the whole chain in one hand and pass it, one section at a time, to the other hand when it has been polished. Never try to polish more than one section at a time and make sure that the sections of chain not being polished are covered by one or other of your hands.

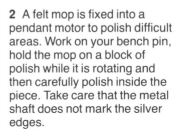

Using a pendant motor
1 Use a brass mop and detergent to give silver a matt finish. Always use a detergent with a brass mop; if you do not, the finish will look rather harsh.

2 A felt mop is fixed into a pendant motor to polish difficult areas. Work on your bench pin, hold the mop on a block of polish while it is rotating and then carefully polish inside the piece. Take care that the metal shaft does not mark the silver edges.

Reticulation

The dictionary definition of reticular is "in the form of a network" and the definition of reticulated is "having veins, fibres or lines crossing like a network, as in a leaf". These definitions accurately describe the appearance of metal after a particular type of heat treatment has been applied, a process that is known as reticulation.

For reticulation to work, the surface of a piece of silver must have a higher melting point than the interior of the piece. This is because the effect is achieved by the silver's surface creasing as the piece is heated: the heat melts the inside of the silver, which flows as a liquid and causes the thin, but unmelted surface to ripple.

The pure silver content of standard silver is 92.5 per cent. The remaining 7.5 per cent is copper and reticulation relies on this "impurity". When standard silver is heated, the copper content oxidizes, turning the surface black when it is cooled in air. When pure silver is heated, no oxides appear and the piece remains a whitish-silver colour.

It is also possible to bring the pure silver to the surface of standard silver. This creates a "sandwich" of two layers of pure silver, with an exterior

melting point of 960°C (1760°F), and an inside layer of standard silver, which has a melting point of 890°C (1635°F). This is done by heating the piece of silver to annealing temperature and then either quenching it in a solution of 1 part sulphuric acid to 10 parts water and rinsing it, or cooling it in water first and then placing it in a warm solution of 1 part sulphuric acid and 10 parts water.

This process is repeated six or seven times to bring the fine silver to the surface. It is important that the temperature does not exceed the point at which annealing takes place or the copper will break through the surface of pure silver that has begun to build up.

As the annealing and quenching process is continued, a layer of fine silver will build up until no

oxidization appears on the metal's surface. It is now time to begin reticulation.

If you do not have two sources of heat, work on the whole piece of silver, heating it just past annealing temperature, and then concentrate your flame hard on one area until the surface begins to move. Then move the flame slowly over the silver, and the surface behind the flame will "ripple" until you have covered the whole piece. It is important that the temperature of the silver is maintained throughout the procedure and that concentrating the flame on one area does not allow the rest of the piece to cool down. If you are working with a single flame, it is probably best to reticulate one small piece at a time, probably no more than about 50 x 30mm (2 x 1¼in).

Throughout the reticulation process the metal is on the point of melting, and there will be times when the silver will actually melt and collapse into holes. This need not necessarily be a disaster, and the holes can often be incorporated into the design. In fact, if you are aiming for a rippled, haphazard effect, a few holes can enhance the appearance of the piece.

SEE ALSO

- Annealing 14–15
- Pickling & quenching 98–99

Bringing silver to the surface
1 Place the silver on the charcoal block and begin to heat it up with soft flame, gradually increasing the heat.

2 Once the silver is hot enough – that is, once it is a deep red – watch the surface carefully until you see that it is beginning to move.

3 Introduce a smaller flame, directing it at one small area and moving it along the length of the silver.

4 Continue to watch as you draw the smaller flame along the surface of the silver and keep the larger flame steady because it keeps the whole piece at the same temperature.

7 Place some soda crystals in an oven-proof dish and cover them with boiling water to make an alkaline solution. Place the piece in this solution, which you can keep warm by placing the dish in a pan of hot or boiling water.

5 Withdraw the flame when the surface is stippled and allow the piece to cool for a while before quenching it in water.

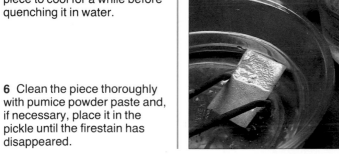

6 Clean the piece thoroughly with pumice powder paste and, if necessary, place it in the pickle until the firestain has disappeared.

8 Clean thoroughly with pumice powder paste.

Riveting

Riveting is a useful way of joining pieces of metal with another piece of metal, wood or plastic. If a riveted join is to be tight, the rivet should be placed directly through the pieces and spread at either end to give a tight fit. If you want the join to have a degree of flexibility you can fit washers between each layer before the rivet is spread.

The wire used to make a rivet should fit neatly into the hole. If the diameter of a rivet is too small, the ends cannot be spread enough to hold it in the hole. In addition, the wire will be able to bend slightly inside the hole and will not, therefore, hold it properly.

A rivet should always be spread into a countersunk area around the top of a hole. If it is appropriate, the rivet can be soldered to the bottom piece and the other pieces placed over it, finishing with the top piece which has a countersunk hole.

To make a rivet, the wire is pushed through all the pieces. The wire should protrude by approximately 1mm (1/32in) from the metal, and both ends should be filed straight. A pointed punch is then placed in the centre of one end of the wire and hammered slightly, while the base is supported either on a small anvil or on the end of a flat punch, which is held in a vice. The piece is then turned over and the other end of the wire is similarly hammered with a pointed punch.

If you need to remove a rivet, file off the head, place the other end over a hole or hold the piece in a vice, so that the rivet can be pushed through. Place the pointed punch in the centre of the rivet and tap it gently until it comes through at the other side.

Using taps and dies

Very small taps and dies, similar to those used for fine jewellery work, need careful handling. A hole slightly smaller than the hole you wish to screw into should be drilled through the metal. The tap should be placed in a small hand drill and worked very slowly through the hole. Ideally it should be given a quarter- or at most a half-turn and then reversed to remove the swarf that the cut has made. If the tap is forced through the metal, it is likely to break and to get stuck in the hole.

The wire to make the screw should be fractionally larger than the first hole that was drilled in the metal. It should be placed squarely in the die and the die then turned around the wire, taking it as far up as necessary. Either undo the die to remove the wire or turn the die the other way and unscrew the wire.

If you need a head on the screw, it must be soldered on. This can be done before the wire is put in the die, with any excess solder around the head being filed away first. This does, however, mean that it will not be possible to take the thread all the way up the wire.

To put a head on a screw that has a thread all the way up, paint a paste of rouge powder to within a millimetre of one end of the screw and allow it to dry completely. Use a tiny paillon of easy solder to solder the head and screw together and file a groove across the head after it has been soldered.

1 Centre punch; **2** and **3** small taps and handle with die plate.

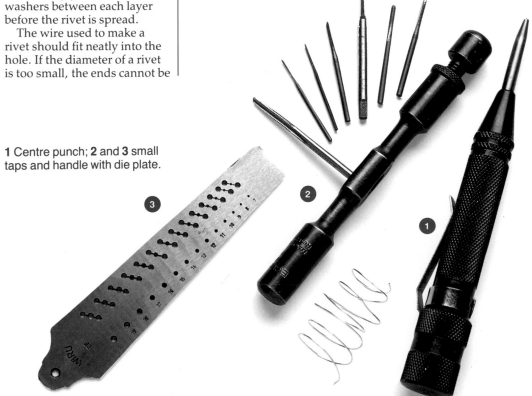

2 Countersink the outside edges of the holes so that the head of the rivet has somewhere to sit. You can do this with a drill bit that is a few sizes larger than the original hole.

Riveting sections together
1 Assemble all the parts to be riveted, then line them all up correctly before drilling the holes for the rivets. Use wire that fits the drilled holes exactly.

3 Place the wire rivet through the piece and cut or file the ends so that they protrude by approximately 1mm (1/32in) above the surface of the metal. Use a pointed punch to mark the centre of the rivet and spread it slightly by hitting the punch gently with a jeweller's hammer or a small ballpien (ballpeen) hammer.

4 Use a flat-nosed punch to spread the head of the rivet on both sides.

5 You can use the flat head of a small hammer to spread the rivet, but be careful that you do not mark the metal with it.

7 The rivet will seem to disappear completely if the head is spread sufficiently for it to fill the countersunk area.

6 Carefully file away any excess rivet.

Riveting links of a chain
1 Drill holes in the links for the rivets and countersink the holes at the top and bottom of the chain.

2 You will need to insert a small washer between the two links to allow some movement. Cut a small piece of chenier that will fit snugly over the rivet.

3 Place the two pieces together and cut the rivet to size. As in the previous procedure, the rivet should protrude by about 1mm (1/32in) both above and below. Spread the head of the rivet with a punch.

4 Alternatively, spread the rivet head by tapping it gently with a jeweller's hammer.

Taps and dies

1 Choose a drill bit that is fractionally smaller than the hole you want to tap and drill through all the pieces that are to be screwed together.

3 Place the corresponding die piece in the handle. The wire for the screw should just fit the hole in the die as it is tightened. Slowly push the whole handle around the wire, hold the wire firmly in your other hand and allow the die to do the work.

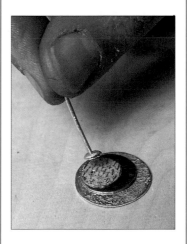

Riveting a pin to a brooch
Cut a piece of wire to fit snugly through the fichu joint and support the lower half of the rivet on the side of a small anvil. Use a punch to spread the head, turn it over and spread the head of the other side.

2 Place the tap in a hand-held drill and very slowly drill the hole. Work a quarter of a turn at a time and turn the drill back anticlockwise each time to get rid of any swarf that is produced by the cut. Tiny taps such as this break easily if they are forced.

4 Screw the pieces together. Cut and file the head of the screw.

Soldering

Precious metals are usually joined together by means of a solder that is compatible with the metal. Soldering is carried out with a gas torch, of which there are several possible types available.

Before metal is soldered it must be perfectly clean, and there should be no signs of oxidization or grease on the surface. In addition, the pieces to be joined should fit as closely together as possible, with no visible gap between them. This is because solder flows by capillary action between close-fitting pieces of metal, and if light is visible between the two pieces, soldering will be difficult. When pieces of gold are to be soldered together, the join must be as tight fitting as possible. If there is a gap of any sort, the solder will run on one side of the join only – gold solder will never "jump" across a gap, although silver solder may occasionally do so.

Fluxes
Solder needs an agent to help it flow, and this agent is called flux. Different kinds of flux should be used with different types of solder and at different temperatures. It prevents any air that is around the join being soldered from oxidizing in the heat from the flame, thereby keeping the metal clean enough for the solder to run and make the join.

Borax The most common, general-purpose borax comes in a cone, which sits in a ceramic dish.

Auflux Also a general-purpose flux, auflux is supplied in liquid form. Use a paintbrush to transfer it to the join.

Tenacity no. 5 Like Easy-flo, this flux comes in powder form and is mixed with water to form a paste. It can withstand much higher temperatures, and it is, therefore, used with metals that require high-temperature solders.

Types of solders
For the projects in this book, silver solder has been used on all the metals, apart from gold and platinum.

Silver solder Silver solder is available in five different grades – enamelling, hard, medium, easy and extra easy – and it is supplied in strips about 45cm (18in) long.

Enamelling This is the solder with the highest melting point, and it requires a temperature of around 810°C (1490°F), which is close to the melting temperature of standard silver, 890°C (1635°F). For this reason, enamelling solder can cause problems. It is, as the name suggests, used on work that is to be enamelled, but not normally for other purposes. Enamel fires at temperatures between 780 and 980°C (1440–1800°F), so the higher the melting point of the solder, the less likelihood there is that the join will come apart in the kiln. In practice, however, hard solder usually withstands lower enamelling temperatures and can be used instead.

Hard The strips of hard solder are about 5mm (¼in) wide. If a piece is to have more than one soldered join, hard solder is the grade to use first, and if a piece has several joins, it is possible, if you are careful, to use hard solder four or five times before using medium or easy solder.

Medium This solder is sold in strips approximately 1.5mm (¹⁄₁₆in) wide. It can be difficult to use because it sometimes seems "sticky" and unwilling to flow easily. It should be used after hard solder but before easy solder.

Easy Strips of easy solder are about 3mm (⅛in) wide, and the solder melts at about 670°C (1240°F). It is used for soldering findings, attachments, jump rings and so on, and it is sometimes used when there is just a single join on a piece – on a simple ring, for example.

Extra easy This kind of solder should be used only as a last resort. It has a very low melting point, and it has a rather yellowish-grey appearance.

Gold solder There is a separate solder for use with each carat of gold. It is sometimes supplied in little sheets, about 35 x 20mm (1¼ x ¾in). Each separate carat is available as easy, medium and hard solder,

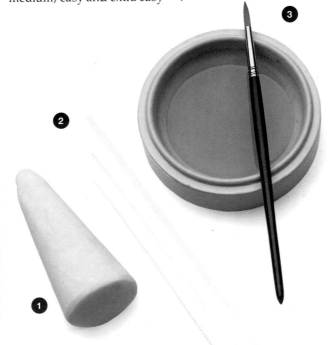

1 Borax cone for making flux; **2** strips of hard, medium and easy solder; **3** Argotec, mixed with methylated spirit and painted onto silver before annealing and/or soldering to prevent fire stain.

and it can be obtained in the same colours as the gold you have used – yellow, red, white and green.

Platinum solder Solder for platinum is available in hard, medium, easy and extra easy forms. Platinum is a very strong metal, which can be worked extremely finely while still retaining a strong structure. Heat is applied only to the area to be soldered. A fine, hot flame is recommended for soldering platinum, and tinted goggles are usually worn because the temperatures are higher than those needed for silver or gold.

Other equipment

Keep a pair of insulated tweezers or a titanium soldering stick in your free hand as you solder. If a piece moves or if a paillon of solder becomes dislodged, you can carefully push it back into place. Do not immerse your insulated tweezers in acid, however. Use brass tongs or tweezers to take the metal into and out of the pickle.

Binding wire is used to hold pieces together so that they can be soldered. Never quench a piece in acid while the binding wire is still in place. Either quench the article in cold water, remove the wire and then pickle in hot acid, or remove the binding wire with snips while the piece is still hot, and then quench in the acid.

Soldering metals

Work that is to be soldered is placed either on a charcoal block or on a heat-resistant soldering block. These can be placed directly on the bench provided they are on some kind of protective metal sheet.

A revolving tray, which can be turned around as soldering progresses, is very useful.

When you are soldering, work in a darkened area. In this way you will be able to see the changing colours of the metal as it is heated.

Flux must be applied carefully onto and into the area to be soldered. For example, if you are soldering a ring, the two sides should be sprung apart slightly so that the flux can be applied to each side before being allowed to spring back into place. The appropriate grade and quantity of solder should be cut into tiny paillons and placed in the flux. If the paillons of solder need to be held at an awkward angle for soldering, a little "teepol" or detergent can be added to the flux to help hold the solder in position. If you hammer or roll silver solder before use, you will be able to cut even smaller paillons.

The work should be heated gently at first. Always play the flame over the whole piece. When soldering silver, the entire article needs to be at soldering temperature before the solder will begin to flow. When soldering gold, concentrate on the area to be soldered to make the solder flow once the entire piece is hot. If you need to "un-solder" a piece, tie the article to a charcoal soldering block with binding wire. Apply flux to the join to be separated and heat the metal until the solder is about to flow. Then use insulated tweezers to pick up or separate the pieces.

Colour changes

It is important to be able to recognize the colour changes that occur in different metals

so that you will know when the solder is about to flow. The following are guidelines only for the colours of different metals when hard solder will flow:

- Silver – bright cherry red
- 9 carat gold – alarming red
- 18 carat gold – alarmingly bright orange-red.

Soldering chains

It is possible to solder several sections of a chain that has been connected up at the same time. Lay up to four sections flat across the charcoal block so that none of the joins to be soldered touch any other part of the links. Cut up paillons of the solder you will be using and place them in the borax flux, which should not be too wet. Use fine stainless steel tweezers or a fine paintbrush

1 Third hand – tweezers in stand used to hold pieces in place while soldering;
2 binding wire; **3** boxwood sawdust.

to pick up the paillons. Paint flux through the four joins and lay a paillon of solder across each join. Solder one section at a time and allow to air cool or quench in water before preparing the next four sections to be soldered. Pickle the whole chain when you have finished soldering.

If you want to solder single jump rings between sections of chain, flux and solder each ring individually. Hold the ring in a pair of insulated tweezers so that it stands on its own, with the rest of the chain hanging down from it, or lay the ring on a charcoal block. Place the ring so that the join is uppermost. Flux and lay a paillon of solder across the top. Only heat the ring you are soldering, by starting at the base of it and bringing the flame to the top and up to the solder. If you just heat the top of the ring around the solder, the solder will melt first and form a ball on one side of the join, and it is then unlikely that the join will solder successfully. It will need realigning so that the two sides are touching again, and you will need to reflux before heating and resoldering.

SEE ALSO

- Annealing 14—15
- Pickling & quenching 98—99

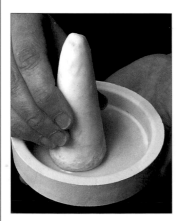

Soldering metals
1 Put a little water in the bottom of the dish and grind the flat end of a borax cone until a whitish paste is produced.

2 Paint the borax paste between the two pieces of metal you want to join.

3 Use a pair of tin snips to cut a strip of solder about 20mm (¾in) lengthwise and then cut across the strips to make paillons. Place the paillons to be used in the borax and keep the others in a dish, clearly marked "easy", "hard" and so on as appropriate.

4 Use the tip of a paintbrush to pick up and place a paillon just below or on the join.

5 Place the piece on a charcoal block and heat it gently, making sure that the paillon of solder stays in position. The heat is likely to make the water in the borax paste bubble, so use a pair of insulated tweezers or a titanium stick to reposition the paillon if necessary.

6 Watch the solder becoming shiny as it melts and runs along the join. Remove the flame and allow the piece to cool for a few seconds.

7 Quench the piece in pickle and rinse in water.

Soldering chains

1 You need to isolate each link of a chain before soldering. You can do this either by holding the link to be soldered in a "third hand" or by laying the chain out flat on a charcoal block and soldering a few links at a time. Always make sure that the areas to be soldered are not in contact with any other metal.

2 Here a "third hand" is being used to hold the ring.

2 Direct a small flame on a single link. It will heat up quickly and allow the solder to flow without affecting the solder on the other links.

Joining pieces

1 Use a piece of binding wire to hold the two pieces you want to join firmly together and twist the wire with flat-nosed pliers to tighten it. Adjust alignment if necessary. Hold the piece in a pair of insulated tweezers and paint the join with flux before placing the paillons around the area to be joined.

Stick soldering

1 Instead of paillons, a long strip of solder, painted with flux, is held in insulated pliers so that it can be fed all the way around the area to be joined.

2 When the soldering temperature is reached, feed the stick solder into the work, taking care to remove it when enough has been fed in.

Stamping and Making Blanks

Impressions can be made in metal in several ways, but all involve the use of some sort of punch that has been fashioned into the pattern required in the metal. The time taken to make a tool is well spent when you want to produce several identical pieces. Stamped metal has an appearance that cannot be achieved in any other way.

Keep some tool steel stock to hand so that you can make a punch when you need it rather than having to buy a little bit every time. You may need to have access to a grinder or you can fit a round carborundum stone to your polishing motor. Alternatively, use a file to model the steel and round off the edges, while the inside edges can be filed away with a burr attachment on the pendant motor. Punches are made from round, square or six-sided stock up to about 20mm (¾in) in diameter. Stock that is larger than this is difficult to heat properly without special equipment, and you should not, in any case, use stock that is too large for your needs. Punches are normally 8–10cm (3½–4in) long.

Keep your punches wrapped in a cloth or in a dry plastic bag so that they do not rust and keep the ends polished.

Metal that is to be stamped should be annealed and should not be too thick, because the thicker the metal the greater the force that is needed to make the depression. Metal that is 0.5–1mm thick is suitable.

Supports

Lead cake Small amounts of lead sheet can be bought from plumbing and building suppliers. Find an old tin, measuring about 14 × 8 × 5cm (5½ × 3½ × 2in), cut up the lead into small pieces and place them in the tin. Heat the lead with a large flame until it melts and leave it to settle and cool. Use a strip of wood to scrape away any impurities that may gather while the lead is molten. When the lead is cold it is ready for use. Impressions made by punching into the lead can be easily erased by heating it once more.

Pitch Although it can be a little hard, pitch can be used as a backing for a punch.

Anvil or flat bed A stamped impression can be made into metal by placing it on a flat metal surface. Hold the punch on the metal and give it a sharp blow with a hammer. This will not form the pattern or design on the other side, although it may leave a mark, even though it does leave a fairly deep impression of the stamp on the top surface of the metal. Hall marking is a classic example of this kind of stamping. If you are making a tool to use to impress a mark, remember that the edge of the tool will leave a mark unless it has been filed away or unless the impression of the pattern itself stands proud of the punch by 1–2mm.

1 Sandbag; **2** punch with patterned head; **3** stainless steel blanks – cut and used with the RT blanking system.

Casting sand This very fine, cohesive material can be packed into a container and used to back metal that is to be embossed. The metal is placed face down in the sand, the punch is placed on the back of the metal and hit with a hammer. The metal will be depressed into the sand as the punch is hit, pushing the pattern through to the front. You can make a metal block to locate the punch so that a second blow can be struck without the punch moving out of line.

Leather pouch or sandbag A round leather pouch, filled with sand, gives a firm but malleable backing into which metal can be hit.

Punches

Wooden moulds Metal can be punched into a turned or carved wooden mould. Alternatively, a male wooden mould can be made in conjunction with a female one, so that the metal can be put between the two pieces and the whole thing squeezed slowly in a vice.

Metal stamps and dies Because they must be very precise, metal stamps and dies are produced by professional companies. If you are going to be making a large number of pieces with a single pattern it is worth considering having a stamp made for you.

RT Blanking System This is a special method for reproducing a large number of identical two-dimensional pieces. Although it takes a little getting used to, the system does work well. It is, basically, a hand-operated fret saw, except that the table through which the saw passes can be tilted at a range of angles according to the thickness of the metal being cut to create the model. A chart accompanying the system is used to get the angle correct. The blanks are cut from stainless steel, which, because of its strength, can be used for at least 500 blankings. The blade of the saw is tightened by a long screw arm, which is fiddly to do at first, but it does work, so it is worth persevering with it. Follow the instructions to make the first cut-out shapes and you will quickly see how you can adapt the system to create your own designs. You may find it easier to cut half a design first, then to turn it over and cut the other half rather than cutting the whole design at once.

SEE ALSO

- Annealing 14–15
- Soldering 112–115

Making a punch
1 Heat a piece of tool steel about 10cm (4in) long and with a diameter of about 15mm (⅝in). Pack charcoal blocks around it and use a large torch.

Heat the steel until it is cherry red, hold it at that colour for a few seconds and then allow it to cool naturally.

4 Hammer the punch lightly into a lead block to check the appearance and make any refinements you wish – filing away sharp edges, for example – then clean the end with wet and dry papers before polishing it on the mop. Rub some soap over the polished end to protect it while it is being "tempered".

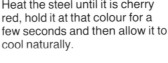

2 File or grind the pattern of your choice into the end of the steel bar.

3 Reheat the whole piece until it is bright red, then quench it in water to harden it.

5 Reheat the end one-third of the steel bar until it becomes a deep yellow. This tempers or just softens the pattern on the punch, which might otherwise become too brittle and liable to chip.

6 Place the silver on the lead block, protecting the underside of the silver with muslin, leather, calico or soft paper so that lead particles are not left in the metal. These would burn into the metal during annealing. Hold the punch upright and give it a sharp blow with a heavy hammer.

7 Build up a stock of individual punches so that you can make repeating patterns on earrings, cuff links, badges and so forth.

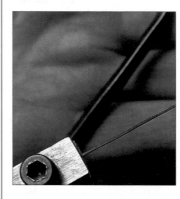

Making blanks using the RT System
1 Position the saw blade so that the teeth point downwards but sideways in the saw. Do up the blade with the Allen key provided.

2 Tighten the blade with the long screw that fits through the saw.

3 Use the green chart provided with the saw to adjust the angle of the table. This angle will depend on the thickness of the steel sheet you are using, so you should measure that first.

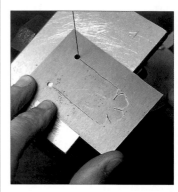

4 Hold the saw loosely at the base and let it fall through the steel as you saw around the pattern.

5 Press the pattern through the steel sheet with your finger and thumb.

9 Reverse the position of the silver in the jig to prepare for the second cut.

10 Place the silver/steel sandwich between the two flat plates as before to produce the blank.

6 Slide the silver sheet up between the two pieces of steel, making sure that you push enough silver into place to allow the second cut of the pattern.

8 One side of the pattern is now cut.

7 Place the silver/steel sandwich between two flat plates and hit it sharply with a heavy hammer.

11 You can now make as many pieces, all exactly the same, as you wish.

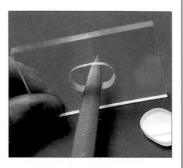

Embossing

1 Pierce the pattern you want to emboss in a sheet of stainless steel. Place the pierced pattern, your template, on a piece of annealed silver about 0.6mm thick. If you have used a piece of stainless steel that is more than 1mm (1/32in) thick, use a thicker piece of silver. Pass the two through the rolling mill so that the steel presses into the silver.

2 The stainless steel template can be used again and again.

4 Use an oval file to neaten the inside of the "male" side of the block.

6 Place the "female" oval on the back of the silver that is to be embossed and use either a fly press to push the "female" part into the silver, using a rubber block as backing, or use the "safe" jaws of your vice, with a rubber block on one side so that the silver and the "female" dye behind it can be pushed into it. Tighten the vice carefully so that the perspex is pushed into the silver so that the silver is slightly domed.

5 File the "female" part of the block to the shape required for the piece of silver. This is a gently domed, oval shape. Make sure that you leave a clearance that is the same as the width of the metal – 0.6mm in this instance – between the "male" and "female" parts.

3 To make the surround, pierce the desired shape out of a sheet of perspex that is the same thickness as the depth of the finished piece of silver.

7 Now place the silver into the "male" part of the block and place the "female" part on top. Place it in the fly press as before or press them carefully together in "safe" jaws of your vice.

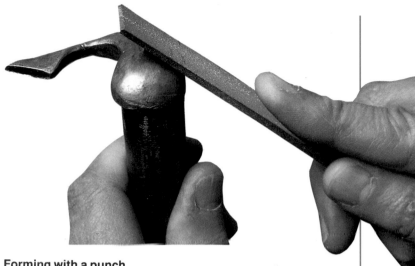

8 The dome will be clearly defined.

9 Use your piercing saw to remove the spare silver from the outside edge of the dome.

Forming with a punch
1 Solder the model of the shape – in this case a fish – to some tool steel and file it to shape. The surface is smoothed and polished.

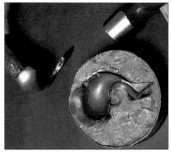

3 The annealed copper sheet is pushed into the depression in the lead with the punch. Repeat this, using a sheet of silver.

2 It can then either be hammered into a cold lead cake or the lead can be heated until it is soft and the punch then carefully placed into it and left to cool with the lead.

10 This bracelet was made by a series of domed pieces, soldered together, with simple stamped pieces between them.

4 The two pieces can be soldered together to create a brooch.

Stone Setting

A stone or cluster of stones is usually the focal point for a piece of jewellery. The wonderful variety of colour, texture and reflective qualities of stones is a constant source of pleasure, inspiration and beauty for both the wearer and the maker.

Many stones are quite tiny, which means that making collets, mounts and settings is a fiddly, difficult task. To begin with, it is a good idea to set some large cabochon stones into rub-over settings, then to practise on a faceted stone of a similar size. In the jewellery trade some craftsmen specialize in making mounts for stones, while others specialize in setting them. If you are using precious stones, you should always consider sending the pieces to a specialist setter so that you can be certain that it has been properly set.

There will, however, be many occasions when it will be appropriate and when you will wish to do your own setting.

Stones can be set singly, in a group or cluster, or in lines. There are two main types. Cabochon stones, which have a smooth overall surface, can be oval, round, tear-drop or curved in some other shape. Faceted stones have flat faces cut into them, in a variety of sizes and at a variety of angles, and these allow the light to be reflected in different ways.

There are two types of faceted stone. The first group includes predominantly straight-sided stones. The second group includes predominantly cone-shaped stones.

Stones have different degrees of hardness and softness, which affects the ways they are set. Soft stones – opals and turquoises, for example – are vulnerable to knocks and scratches and need a more protective setting than a hard stone such as a diamond or ruby, which could be given a lighter, more open setting.

Rub-over settings

Cabochon stones are usually given rub-over settings. The bezel, which is the metal surrounding the stone, should extend just over the first section of the slope to hold the stone in place. If you are uncertain, measure the height of the stone and make the bezel about one-third of that measurement.

The bezel can be soldered directly to a metal backing, on which the stone sits, or a "bearer" wire can be soldered to the lower half of the bezel to make a ledge. The stone sits on the ledge and is not in contact with the background metal.

Bezels can be decorated by having patterns pierced along their length before they are soldered into a round or oval shape. Leave at least 2mm (1/16in) unpierced around the top of the bezel so that there is some substance to the metal when it is pushed down over the stone.

Estimating the length of the bezel for a round stone
To estimate the length of the bezel for a round stone, do the following calculation:

Diameter + thickness of metal x π

Estimating the length of the bezel for an oval stone
To estimate the length of the bezel for an oval stone, do the following calculation:

Length + width ÷ 2 + thickness of metal x π

To be absolutely certain, you can allow a little extra and pierce it away if necessary. Even if the bezel is a little large, it will still push down neatly onto the stone.

Setting a cabochon
1 One way of finding the outside measurement of a stone is to draw around it with a pencil. Use a small piece of removable adhesive "tak" to hold it down if necessary.

Faceted stones
A faceted stone has a table, a girdle and a culet. The area between the girdle and the table is known as the crown and the area from the girdle to the culet is known as the pavilion.

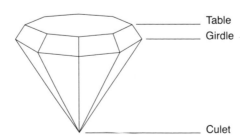

Table
Girdle

Culet

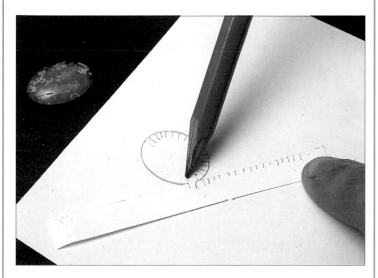

2 Cut a strip of paper and place one of the long edges against the edge of the drawn oval, using a pencil to mark both the strip and the oval. Move the strip around the oval a little at a time, marking it each time, until you have marked the complete length. Add onto this figure 1.5 times of the metal you will use for the bezel.

3 Use dividers to measure the height of the bezel. It should go over the curve of the stone. Draw the dividers down a strip of metal to mark this measurement and then cut it to length. Bend into an oval and solder.

4 Smooth the base of the oval on a flat file.

5 Place the oval on a sheet of silver, flux around the base and solder the two together.

6 Pierce away the silver from around the outside of the oval.

7 Tidy the edge with a file and finish off with wet and dry papers. Solder the setting to the piece, and polish and finish the piece before beginning to set the stone.

8 Use a pusher to lever the bezel over the stone. Begin at one side, then push down the opposite side. Continue in this way, making sure that the stone is securely held, before finally pushing it down all the way round.

9 Use a curved, polished burnisher to smooth the bezel.

10 Tidy the top edge of the setting with a spitstick, which can be used to level off any uneven areas.

123

Setting faceted stones

Faceted stones can be mounted in an open claw-type setting, set in chenier, set into collets made from wire or sheet, which are then pierced and filed to allow light to reflect from the stone, or set flush with the metal in pave settings. When you are using any of these settings, you must accurately measure the stone at the girdle and also the height from the girdle to the table and the overall length. Use a vernier or dixième tool to do this accurately.

You can buy ready-made collets from your metal dealer or you can make them yourself by bending up a sheet into a cone, which is suitable for cone-shaped stones, or by bending up wire or sheet to form rectangles, squares, triangles and so on for straight-sided stones.

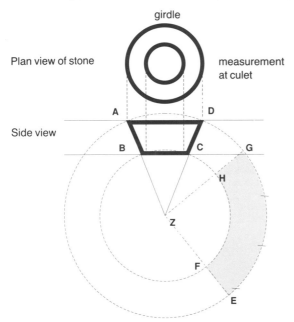

girdle

Plan view of stone

measurement at culet

Side view

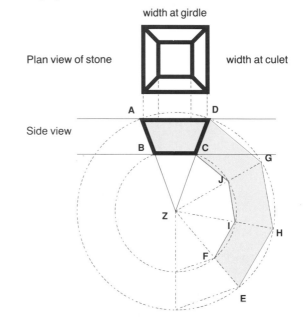

width at girdle

Plan view of stone

width at culet

Side view

Drawing the pattern for a round cone mount

1 Measure the diameter of the stone at the girdle. Use this measurement to draw A–D.
2 Measure the vertical distance from the girdle to the culet, allowing extra if you are making claws as part of the cone = AB – DC.
3 Use these measurements to draw lines, continuing AB and DC to meet at Z.
4 Draw a circle, centre Z, with a radius DZ.
5 Draw a second circle, centre Z, with a radius CZ.
6 Use dividers to measure the distance AD, and mark this dimension on the outer circle starting at a point G three and one-seventh times (π), and mark this point E.
7 Draw in line GZ.
8 Draw in line EZ.
9 Make points H and F on the inner arc.
The shape bounded by GEFH is the flat cone. Transfer this to the metal and cut out the shape. Anneal the metal and shape the cone on a tapered mandrel. Offer up the stone to the cone and adjust the shape if necessary. Solder the seam. The cone is now ready to be pierced or to have claws or a pattern on the bottom filed on it. Solder a wire ring to the bottom of the cone after it has been cut and filed to shape.

Establishing the measurements for straight-sided stones

1 Measure the square stone along one side = AD.
2 Measure the height from girdle to culet (allow extra if you are making claws or a rub-over) = AB and DC.
3 Extend lines AB and DC to meet at Z.
4 Draw a circle, centre Z, with a radius DZ.
5 Draw a circle, centre Z, with a radius CZ, and draw an arc CF.
6 For a square stone:
Measure the side of your stone (ie AD) with dividers and mark this measurement three times on the outer circle finishing at E.

For a rectangular stone:
Work as for the square stone but measure both the long and short sides of the rectangle. The measurement AD and GH will be the long side; the measurement DG and HE will be the short sides.
The shaded area within these letters is the flat pattern that can be transferred to the metal. The lines DC, GJ and HI are scored and bent up so that AB can be soldered to EF. The mount can then be filed or decorated as wished and outside claws can be soldered to each corner to hold the stone.

Making a claw setting

Claw, or prong, settings can be made from sheet metal or wire, and they can be round, triangular, square or rectangular in section. The essence of a claw or prong is that the stone is held in the claw. A little nick is made in the claw on the inside, which is then bent down over the stone to hold it in place. A round stone needs three or more claws to hold it, and a square or rectangular stone should be held on all four corners. The culet should not come below the base of the setting.

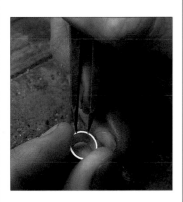

Making a claw setting

1 Make a plain collet using the technique outlined opposite. If you are setting an oval, make a round collet to the correct diameter and use parallel pliers to push it into shape. Use dividers to mark the positions for the claws on the top edge of the collet.

2 With one side of the dividers on the top edge of the collet, carefully mark depth lines on the outside of the collet.

3 Using these lines, mark the design for the claws freehand, using a pencil or fine black pen. Any wholly enclosed areas of pattern can be tackled by drilling a small hole in the centre of the design and threading the saw blade through the hole so that the design can be accurately pierced out from within.

4 Pierce out the claws, working from the top. Ensure that any areas of open work are not pushed out of shape.

5 Cut a location notch inside the top of each claw – the girdle of the stone will sit in these notches. So that they will bend more easily, file the top outside edge of each claw so that it tapers slightly.

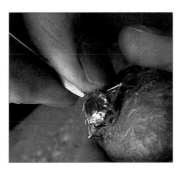

6 Solder the collet to the desired position on the ring shank and finish and polish the ring. Place the ring in a ring stick, sit the stone in position and use a brash pusher to push the tops of the claws over the stone. Work first on one side then on the opposite side and make sure that the table of the stone remains horizontal.

Pavé setting

Stones are sometimes set in clusters or in a line very close to each other, a method known as pavé setting. Cut a slightly tapered hole for the stone so that the girdle of the stone will sit just below the surface of the metal. You can then begin to raise the grains. Push the half-round scorper into the edge of the metal a little way from the edge of the stone, holding it at an angle of 45 degrees to the metal. The metal that is pushed forward in this way causes a bump to appear over the girdle, and it is this that holds the stone in place. The combined effect of stones set in this way is one of uniform lustre.

Texturing

There are many more ways of finishing off a piece of work than by polishing. This is often an appropriate way to complete a piece, but there are lots of interesting ways of texturing the surface of the metal to make it reflect the light in different ways, to emphasize particular parts of the piece or to give a crisp, sharp look to a piece of modern jewellery.

When you are designing a piece, take the finished appearance into account from the start, because texture and surface finish are often added

Texturing
1 Brass brush used with detergent; **2** burrs for use with the pendant motor; **3** graded wet and dry paper; **4** muslin square for use with the rolling mill.

before the piece is assembled or soldered.

All kinds of interesting shapes and patterns can be imprinted on metal by passing it through a rolling mill with fabric, patterned metal, paper, cotton wool or even string. The rollers are made of stainless steel, and you must take care that you do not use anything that will mark them, or every piece that you subsequently pass through them will be spoiled. Although the rollers can be reground professionally, this is both expensive and inconvenient.

Using a pendant motor
Apart from all its other uses, a pendant motor can be fitted with a range of shaped and graded metal burrs, cutters and grinders.

Before you work on a carefully finished piece, try out the different burrs and cutters on pieces of scrap metal so that you learn to control the tool. You will find that it slips quite easily.

When you use a pendant motor to add texture, take as much care as you do when you

are polishing. Tie back long hair and fold back loose sleeves. Always wear goggles to protect your eyes.

Texturing after polishing
Some textures are applied when everything else on a piece has been finished. If a stone has been included you must take extra care.

To achieve a successful textured finish, all scratches, file marks, solder marks and so forth must be removed first.

Finishing a mixed-metal surface
When one metal or more has been inlaid or added to another, a highly polished finish can lessen the impact of the colour contrast. A matt surface, on the other hand, may enhance the difference.

One way of highlighting the change in colour is by polishing the piece to a gloss finish. Clean away the excess

polish, rinse and dry, then heat the pieces with a gentle flame until it begins to oxidize. Quench it when it has cooled a little. Place the piece in a warm solution of sulphuric acid for a minute or two, remove, rinse and dry. Lightly repolish the piece, then reheat and proceed as before. After repeating the polishing, heating, pickling and rinsing process three or four times, the piece can be finally reheated. If the contrasting metal looks better oxidized, the piece needs no further treatment. Otherwise, pickle it in warm acid, rinse and dry.

Re-texturing after assembly
When a piece of metal has been textured before assembly, part or all of the texture may be accidentally removed when you are cleaning and filing around soldered joints. Clearly, it is best to try to avoid this altogether by using the minimum amount of solder necessary for the job, but if it does happen try re-creating the texture by placing the texturing material you used originally on the work and tapping a small, flat-headed planishing punch around the affected area. If the texture was originally created by direct hammering, use a small, shaped punch.

A piece of jewellery with a textured finish can be given extra definition by highlighting edges or high spots with a burnisher.

SEE ALSO
- Annealing 14–15
- Pickling & quenching 98–99
- Polishing 104–105

1 Some cotton wool is being passed through the mill with a piece of silver. The cotton wool makes the surface of the silver slightly dimpled.

Giving a matt finish
1 Using steel wool with liquid detergent gives a fine, matt finish.

Using a pendant motor
1 Some of the finishes that can be achieved by using different tools in the pendant motor.

Using a hammer
1 Use the round end of a ball pien hammer to give an interesting hammered look. Use regular, smooth blows to keep the metal the same shape, although the method can be used to curve a piece of metal (see Bending, pages 18–21).

2 Use a rusty hammer and place the metal on a rusty anvil. Texture the piece all over, then clean it thoroughly afterwards with pumice paste to remove all particles of iron.

2 Pass a sheet of wet and dry paper through the rolling mill with a piece of silver. The silver will have a "frosted" appearance, but remember that filing away solder will remove the textured pattern.

3 Before the silver was passed through a mill with a piece of muslin, tiny squares of 24 carat gold were fused to the surface.

2 A brass brush, also used with liquid detergent, gives a matt finish. Always use detergent – if you do not, the brass will leave the silver rather dark and unattractive.

2 A steel mop gives an attractive, "frosted" appearance. Always wear goggles when you use a steel mop because bits of steel can fly off.

Using Wire

Silver and gold wire are available in almost any thickness you want.

You can get copper wire simply by removing it from old flexes or by removing the rubber casing from bought lengths of electrical wire. You can also buy copper wire in coils, but it often has a coat of lacquer, which is not desirable when it is used for jewellery making. Copper wire is useful for working out the exact dimensions of a piece and to show how the design will bend up and how much wire will be needed and how thick it should be.

To make working with wire easy, it should be kept annealed. Always use the correct pliers so that the wire is not marked by accident, and make jigs if necessary to bend the wire uniformly (see Bending, pages 18–21).

You can obtain wire of any section – square, round, oval, triangular, D-section or rectangular – and the shapes are made by drawing the wire through heavy industrial rollers. However, you can create your own shaped wire by pulling it through a draw plate. This is a steel plate, measuring 15 or 23 x 2cm (6 or 9 x ¾in) and approximately 5mm (¼in) thick, which has a series of holes in decreasing holes, squares, rectangles and so on in one side. On the other side of the plate the holes are slightly opened to allow the larger wire to be inserted in the hole.

The plate should be held in a vice. Make sure that the jaws of the vice do not overlap any of the holes. By drawing down wire and chenier to widths of your own choice, you can make jump rings to specific sizes, and once you have a selection of jump rings, all kinds of ideas for chains will occur to you (see Chain Making, pages 36–41).

If you need to straighten out a length of wire that has been bent or wound, make sure it is annealed, fasten one end tightly in the vice, hold the other end with a pair of serrated edge pliers and pull tight until you feel it stretch, which means that it is completely straight.

SEE ALSO

- Annealing 14–15
- Bending 18–21
- Chain making 36–41

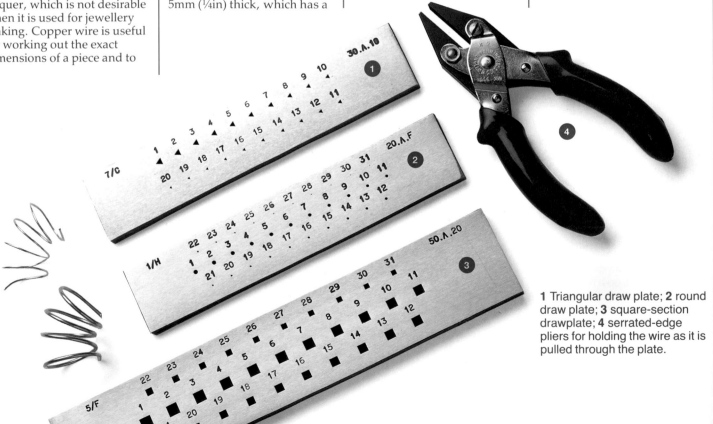

1 Triangular draw plate; 2 round draw plate; 3 square-section drawplate; 4 serrated-edge pliers for holding the wire as it is pulled through the plate.

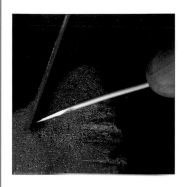

Drawing down wire
1 File the end of the wire into a longish point.

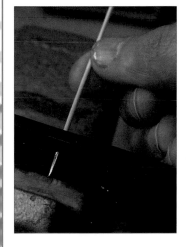

2 Hold the draw plate in a vice, making sure that the jaws do not cover any of the holes in the draw plate, and push the pointed end of the wire through a hole that is just too small to take the rest of the wire.

3 Grip the filed end of the wire with a pair of serrated edge pliers and pull the wire straight through the hole. Repeat this for each decreasing size of hole until the wire is the correct diameter. It will need annealing after three pulls.

Drawing down chenier
1 Find a piece of wire that will fit snugly inside the chenier that is to be made narrower.

2 Melt a little beeswax on the wire and thread it down the chenier. Although the beeswax is not essential, it makes it easier to remove the wire, especially if the chenier is later

3 Place both wire and chenier through a hole in the draw plate that is just smaller than the chenier. Grip both the chenier and the wire with serrated edge pliers and pull them both through the draw plate. Continue until the chenier is the correct size. You will have to anneal the wire and chenier after three or four pulls.

bent or curved. Push the wire through the chenier until only about 5mm (¼in) is visible. File the wire and chenier to a point.

4 Remove the wire by pushing the point through the smooth side of the draw plate. The chenier will not pass through the draw plate as the wire is removed.

Making jump rings

1 Place a metal former in the vice – the smooth end of a drill bit is suitable for this, but make sure that the drilling end is either protected with masking tape or is held in the "safe" jaws of a vice. Hold one end of a piece of annealed wire with a pair of serrated edge pliers.

2 Wind the wire up the former, keeping each turn as close as possible to the preceding one.

4 Place the piercing saw at an angle across the tape and pierce through both the tape and the wire.

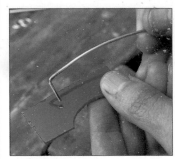

Making a spiral

1 When you make a spiral from wire that is too thick to wind easily in a pair of pliers, bend the end of the wire to a right angle and place it through a hole that has been drilled either in a sheet of metal or in thick perspex. The wire should just fit the hole.

3 Wrap adhesive tape around the wire and the former.

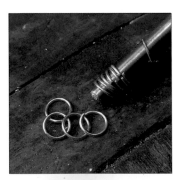

5 The rings will be cut at the right angle, which means that you will not have to tidy the ends with a file. They should sit neatly and close to each other.

2 Fasten the end of the wire tightly in the vice.

3 Use the metal or perspex as a flat plate to start winding the spiral

4 Remove the spiral from the perspex and cut away the piece that was held in the vice.

Making a helix
You can make the spiral into a helix by pushing through from the back with a tapered punch.

Twisting wire
Round wires twisted together can be used as a decorative border around a setting for a cabochon stone or around the top and bottom edges of rings and bangles. Square, rectangular and triangular section wires can be twisted by themselves to create effective edging, although round and oval wires must be twisted with another wire to look effective. You can also use different sections together, either twisting them separately before twisting them together or twisting them all together.

Before bending wire to shape, run solder along the length. If you do not, the twists will open out and loosen. Flux needs to be applied along the whole length of twisted wire, and paillons of solder should be positioned every few millimetres so that the whole piece is evenly soldered. Try not to use too much solder or the twisted wire will look heavy and overworked.

Twisting wire
1 Make a metal hook and fasten it into a hand drill. Take a long piece of annealed wire and bend it in half. Fix the two ends into a vice – it doesn't matter if they are flattened, but they must be held securely. Hook the loop end over the hook in the drill.

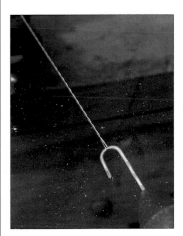

2 Hold the wire straight and wind the handle of the drill smoothly until you are happy with the amount of twist in the wire.

Twisting sections in a length of wire

1 Use dividers to mark on square or rectangular section wire where the twists are to be.

2 Use tape to mask the areas of wire that are not going to be twisted, then place the first section in the vice.

Twisting more than one wire

1 A length of square section wire is being twisted with two lengths of round wire. Solder all three together at one end.

2 Hold the soldered end in the chuck of the hand drill and fasten the other ends in a vice. Wind the handle of the drill until you have the correct twist.

3 Hold the second, protected section with serrated edge pliers and twist the wire four or five times.

4 This piece of silver wire has separate twisted sections along its length.

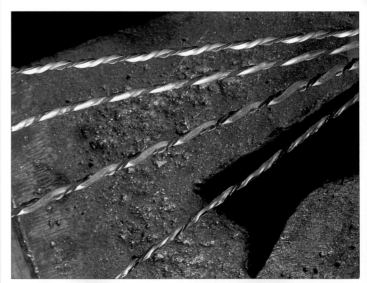

3 Copper and silver wire can be twisted together as shown here (from the top): the copper wire was twisted first, then twisted with silver; after twisting, the wires were pulled through a round draw plate; the copper was twisted first, but less twist was put on the wire, and the whole piece was slightly flattened with a hammer; the twisted wires were pulled through a square section draw plate.

Working with fine or cloisonné wire

This fine wire, between 0.25 and 0.35mm ($\frac{1}{1000}$ and $\frac{1}{100}$in) thick, is made specifically for enamelled cloisonné work (see Enamelling, pages 52–59). It is supplied in reels in lengths of about 20 metres (65 feet).

It can be difficult to anneal cloisonné wire with a torch, because the wire nearest the flame is liable to melt while the rest of the coil is heated. The best method is to cut off the required length from the reel and coil it loosely into a clean shoe polish or tobacco tin. You can then place the tin in a kiln, heated to about 600°C (1110°F), for a minute or two. Only anneal fine wire if it is to be used as shown below. It is not necessary to anneal wire that is to be used for enamelling.

This kind of wire can also be used to make fine "lace-type" and knitted work, and there are some beautiful examples of jewellery made primarily from knitted or crocheted wire, including pieces made by Mary Lee Hue.

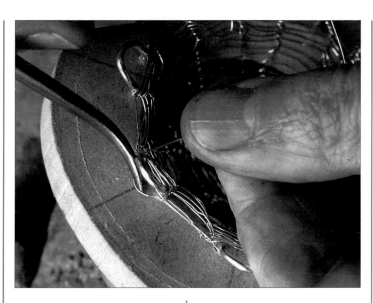

4 Use a smooth crochet hook or a curved burnisher to lift the first wire up and over the second and then over the top of the loop so that it drops into the centre hole.

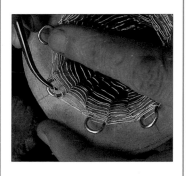

5 Continue to work around the circle, placing one wire over the next, and pushing the inside down as necessary.

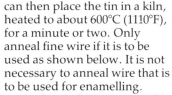

2 Use half-round pliers to form eight loops. Hammer each loop into place and bend over the tops slightly with the half-round pliers.

3 Make a double turn of fine wire around one side of a loop to start off. Take the wire around the back of each loop until you are back at the first loop.

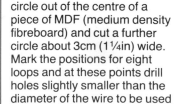

Knitting with wire

1 Use annealed cloisonné wire with a diameter of 0.25–0.3mm ($\frac{10}{1000}$ and $\frac{11}{1000}$in). Cut a circle out of the centre of a piece of MDF (medium density fibreboard) and cut a further circle about 3cm (1¼in) wide. Mark the positions for eight loops and at these points drill holes slightly smaller than the diameter of the wire to be used for the loops.

6 To finish, remove the piece from the frame and fit jump rings through the loops so that you can attach magnetic ends. Wrap the ends neatly around each other and snip them off.

THIS SECTION CONTAINS a wide range of jewellery to inspire and excite the artist in you. It is divided into three main sections—metals, stones and mixed media—and part of the fascination of jewellery making is discovering how the materials and techniques overlap.

There are fantastically varied works from top international designers. These works feature a variety of materials and metals, and show the techniques discussed in the first part of the book used to wonderful effect.

Designing and making jewellery like this takes both skill and time. It also requires patience and an understanding of how materials can be used. But perhaps one of the main attributes of jewellery making is a feel for the colours, textures and shapes that work well together.

Most of the jewellery illustrated here uses several techniques, and as you look at the pieces, you will see how the different methods have been chosen to suit the materials. As you gain experience, you will learn which metals and stones look best together. It is only by seeing the basic materials and techniques used in challenging and surprising ways that you can appreciate the enormous potential that is open to you.

Themes

Metals

Most craft jewellery is made from silver, which is at its best when it is used with other metals, particularly small amounts of a high carat gold. When they are combined, the two metals seem to bring out the best qualities of each other. Because it is so popular, jewellery designers are always looking for new ways of working with silver to produce interesting surfaces and finishes, neat ways of combining different techniques and original ways of introducing colour. Some of the designs illustrated in this section are so successful that it is almost impossible to discern where one technique overlaps with another and where different materials have been used.

The amazingly subtle colours that can be achieved by anodizing titanium, niobium or aluminium are enhanced by the exciting designs that explore the full potential of the metal. Although these metals have little intrinsic value, the ways in which they can be used to create striking pieces show that value is not always monetary. Chemical treatments – patinating copper, for example – can be used to produce some wonderfully attractive yet inexpensive pieces.

Gold has unrivalled qualities. Its lustre, colour and sheen make it one of the most desirable of metals, but its cost does mean that most of us can use it only occasionally. As you look at the pieces in these illustrations, I hope you will feel inspired to consider using the king of metals to make a special piece for yourself, just so that you can discover for yourself the pleasure of working with such a responsive material.

◀ **EARRINGS • Ann Marie Shillito**
The pieces were made from triangles of aluminium, cut to size on a guillotine, and anodized and dyed with proprietary dyes. The triangles were drilled and the ear wires fitted before the top corner was bent down to hold the wire firmly.

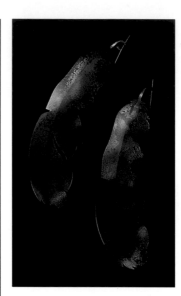

▲ **PENDANT • Jane Adam**
This pendant is made of anodized aluminium, and colours were then applied by monoprinting and painting. The paints created a resist to the black dye that was used for the background colour. A layer of 22 carat gold was applied to the inside of the pendant, and the chain is oxidized silver.

◀ **BROOCHES • Ann Marie Shillito**
A pair of feather-shaped brooches made of anodized titanium. The designer worked by transferring the feather design to a CAD (computer aided design) program, which was then used to laser-cut limited quantities of the brooches. The integral pin was filed to make it round, and the surface of the brooches was given directional finish before the resists were applied and the metal anodized and formed. Each brooch in the series is individually patterned and coloured.

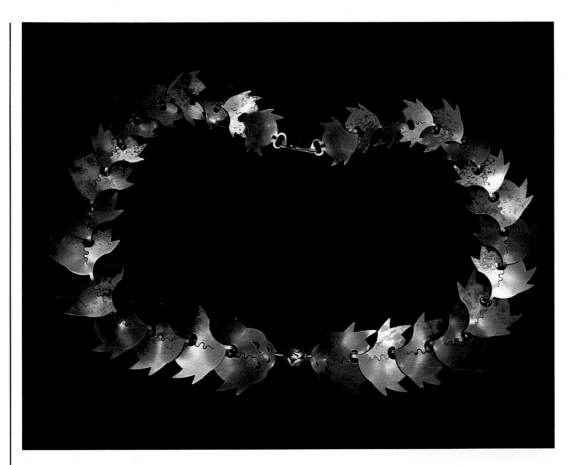

◄ NECKLACE ● **Ann Marie Shillito**
A CAD program was used to laser-cut the pieces of steel and anodized titanium in this necklace. The individual pieces were shaped, anodized and chemically coloured before being linked on a silk thread.

► BROOCH AND EARRINGS ●
Ann Marie Shillito
This matching set was made from anodized niobium and titanium, and they were created by a CAD system and laser cutting. The individual elements were finished before being anodized and shaped, and the various pieces are held together with industrial adhesive. The brooch measures 12.5 x 8.5cm (5 x 3½in).

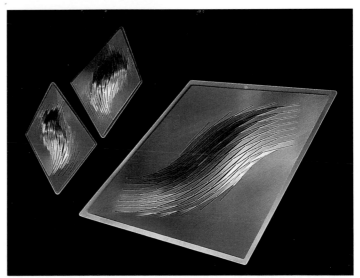

137

▶ **ESSENTIAL COLLECTION** ●
Liz Tyler
All the pieces are made from 14 carat red gold, and the open forms were produced by anticlastic raising techniques. Solid wires were introduced to the tube and the end soldered. The wires were shaped and forged into tight curves, which contrast strongly with the open forms. The depletion gilding technique, which naturally gives rise to the yellow colours, is used to accentuate the forms still further.

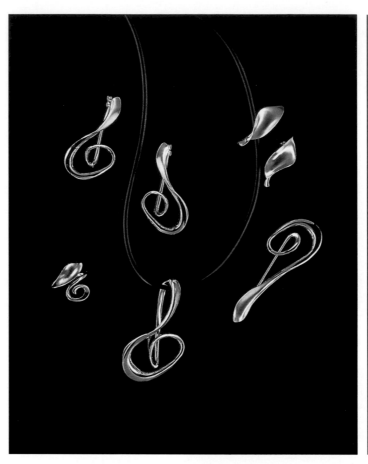

▼ **JAPAN-MOTIFS** ● **Lynda Watson-Abbott**
Gold was soldered onto cast silver for the central section. The surrounding sections were made from sterling silver wire. The design was based on a series of shapes and surfaces observed while in Japan.

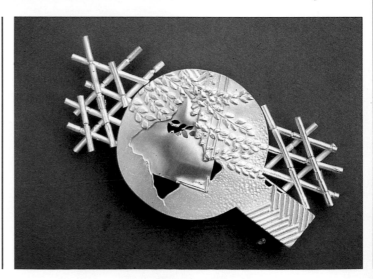

▲ **SILVER BROOCH** ●
Stephen Maer
Cast by lost-wax process. Modelled in carving wax and cast in two pieces in order to avoid deep undercut in rubber mould and achieve high polished finish between the overlapping elements. (45mm x 40mm x 9mm deep)

◄ CUFFLINKS ● **Rebecca Edmunds**
These are made from, variously, fine silver, oxidized silver, 18 carat gold, ebony, slate and semi-precious stones. The techniques employed included bending, soldering, embossing, bezel and tube fitting, and chenier and catch making.

▲ NECKLACE ● **Alexandra Coppen**
Dumortierite bead necklace with unusual 18 carat gold and silver sliding clasp. A 9 carat gold wire on one half of the bead slides into an exactly fitting tube on the other half of the bead.

▲ BYZANTIUM BRACELET ● **Roy**
This piece was made from almost 100g (3½oz) of 18 carat gold, with white and yellow diamonds and a square sapphire. It measures 55 x 216 x 5mm (2⅛ x 8⅝ x ¼in) and involved hinging and stone setting techniques.

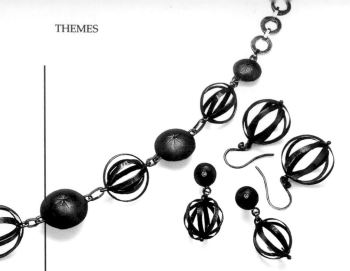

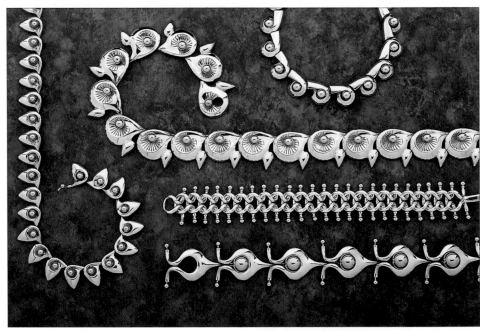

◄ NECKLACE AND EARRINGS ●
Daphne Krinos
Made from oxidized silver and 18 carat yellow gold, there are tiny diamonds in the top section of these earrings. The hollow beads are of forged silver wire, which has been slightly textured. The silver was oxidized and then "scratched" with abrasives. The gold, which is unpolished, was finished with a glass brush to give it a satiny look.

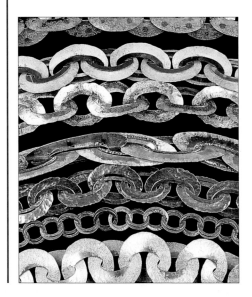

◄ SILVER AND GOLD CHAINS ●
Malcolm Appleby
These 18 carat gold and silver chains were mostly made from wire wound around a mandrel then rolled through mills to make the links oval. The chains were then forged and textured on an anvil to frost the surface.

▲ NECKLACES ● Brett Payne
The designer used a variety of techniques, including forging, casting, buffing, engraving and doming to make these necklaces and bracelets. Note that the links themselves form an integral part of the design.

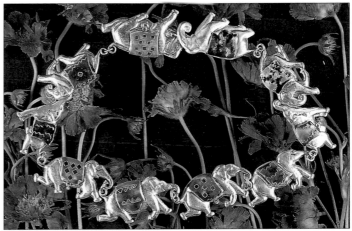

◄ LOCKET ● Jinks McGrath
This silver locket in a gold bezel is enamelled on one side only, the other side being silver with fused paillons of 24 carat gold. The silver chain was fabricated and riveted together. Two rings of twisted silver wire were soldered to each silver dome. The chain can be worn with or without the locket.

▲ NECKLACE ● Avrina Eggleston
A necklace of repoussé elephants, each wearing a transparent enamel carpet.

► BROOCH AND EARRINGS ●
Joanne Gowan
Silver and 18 carat yellow gold were used for this matching set, which involved both repousse and forging techniques.

◄ **EARRINGS AND PIN** • **Astrid Mahrer**
These are made from silver, brass sheet, copper sheet and copper wires, with a steel pin. Perspex moulds were used to chase the silver and brass sheet, which were soldered together, the silver at the front and the brass at the back. The surfaces were punched or drilled and sawn into shapes.

▲ **BANGLE** • **Malcolm Appleby**
Made from a forged sheet of 18 carat gold, this was carved with a hammer and chisel pierced. The carving was then stoned down with Water-of-Ayr stone, polished and engraved. The feather pattern on the swan's neck was achieved by two stab cuts of the graver, one into the other to form a lozenge.

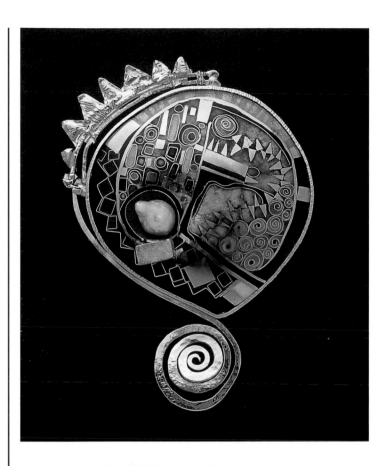

◀ **THE FIRE BIRD ● William Harper**
Made from gold cloisonné enamel on fine silver and gold, this piece incorporates 24, 22, 18 and 14 carat gold, sterling silver and a pearl. The piece measures 88 x 125 x 20mm (3½ x 5 x ¾in). (Courtesy of the Peter Joseph Gallery, New York City)

▶ **FISH TIER ● Janet Pontin**
This enamelled brooch consists of a tiered brooch with small hanging fish. It is made of enamel on copper with silver beads and wire. Powdered enamel was fired onto the copper and opaque enamels were used on top of transparent enamels. The small enamelled copper star was fused into a pre-enamelled layer by firing at extremely high temperatures, and the scraffito technique was used to draw the pattern.

◀ **PARADE ● Linda Pino**
Sterling silver, 14 carat gold and cloisonné enamel were used to make this multi-coloured necklace.

▶ **JUNGLE FANTASY ● Antonia H. Schwed**
This necklace was made by the champlevé technique. The design was etched out with acid, and then the vitreous enamel was fired in the kiln, with both opaque and transparent enamels used on the silver.

▶ PENDANT ● **Clara Vichi**
A resist was applied to the silver used for this piece and the calligraphic pattern hand-scribed through the resist. The silver piece was then etched in acid. Once the resist had been removed, the silver was cleaned, oxidized and varnished and mounted to a wooden disk along with the gold writing. The silver chain was then fitted.

◀ EAST MEETS WEST ● **Jill Newbrook**
The patterns on these photoetched silver pieces were inspired by traditional Japanese textiles. The photoetched design was enhanced by the use of textured, rolled, fine gold, and 18 carat gold wire was added to define the details.

▲ BRACELETS ● Mary Ann Scherr
The images on these silver, bronze, gold and stainless steel bracelets were etched by means of an "instant etch" process, which lends itself equally well to all these metals. The silk-screen process involved takes less than an hour, and it can also be used for piercing designs.

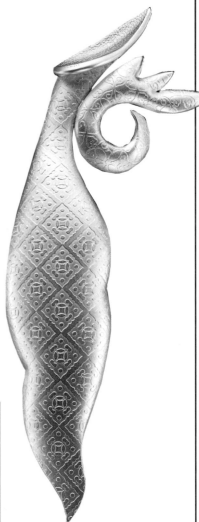

▼ PIN ● Linda Threadgill
This is made of sterling silver and 22 carat gold. The pattern was achieved by photoetching and the hollow form was die-formed and soldered.

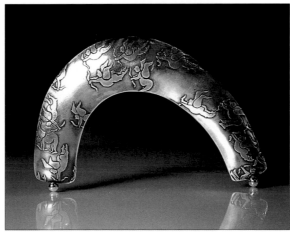

◀ BROOCH ● Sarah Parker-Eaton
This silver brooch, with its etched and oxidized pattern of cherubs, is finished off with little gold balls. It is approximately 8 x 7cm (3¼ x 2¾in).

◄ TRAP ● **Kenneth Earl Rockwell**
This bracelet was mainly fabricated in silver and has some red gold added for contrasting colour. Some of the sections were cast and then set or soldered onto the main piece. The decorative top section is an unusual mixture of enamel and porcelain. The hinge and catch have been cleverly integrated into the design of the piece.

► PENDANT ● **Stephen Maer**
An 18 carat yellow gold and tourmaline pendant. The concave curved surface is decorated with 88 rectangular gold blocks. The blocks are attached by granulation. The edges have been polished, but the upper surface has been left unpolished to emphasise the rectilinear placement of the blocks. The cylindrical green tourmaline has been claw-set into a rectangular bar dividing the two parts of the pendant. (30 x 17 x 7mm deep; 450mm chain.)

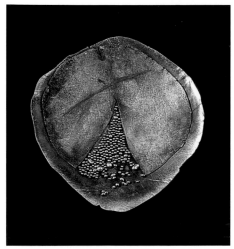

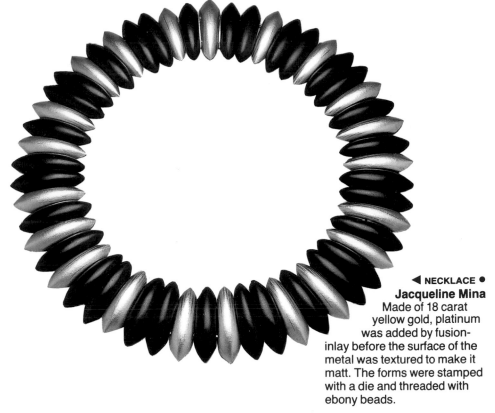

▲ BROOCH • **Harold O'Connor**
This piece measures 4.5cm
(1¾in) in diameter and is made
of 24 and 18 carat gold, silver
and spectrolite using the
granulation technique. The
textured surface was achieved
by passing the silver through a
rolling mill and then fusing the
24 carat gold to the silver sheet.
The gold was then granulated to
the silver.

◀ NECKLACE •
Jacqueline Mina
Made of 18 carat
yellow gold, platinum
was added by fusion-
inlay before the surface of the
metal was textured to make it
matt. The forms were stamped
with a die and threaded with
ebony beads.

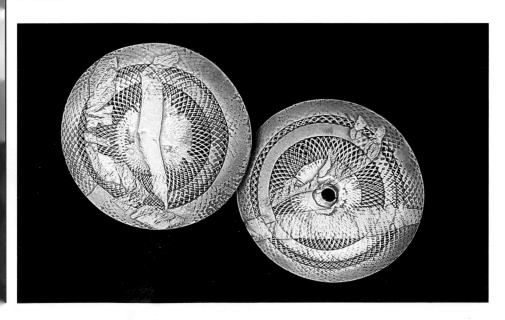

◀ EARRINGS • **Wally Gilbert**
These silver and 22 carat gold
earrings are made from fine
silver wire, 0.35mm in diameter,
which was woven and fused
with standard silver. This was
forged into discs before being
fused with a reducing flame on
charcoal blocks.

◀ BROOCHES ● **Sue Amendolara**
Two sterling silver palmetto brooches with carved ebony and fabricated 24 carat gold foil. The Korean technique of kum boo has been used to fuse gold to silver. The gold dots are made from 18 carat gold.

▶ BANGLE ● **Dorothy Hogg**
This bangle is made from a sterling silver hammered form which has 100 hammered rings that run freely.

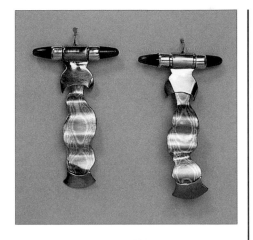

▲ EARRINGS ● **Phebe Allen Blake**
Pink gold and carnelians were used for these earrings, made with the mokumé gané technique.

▲ BROOCHES ● **Jacqueline Mina**
Two brooches, one 62 x 19mm (2¼ x ¾in), the other 65 x 19mm (2½ x ¾in), made from textured and partly oxidized 18 carat yellow gold with platinum inlay.

▶ BROOCH ● **Phebe Allen Blake**
Sterling silver, 14 carat gold and a garnet were used for this penannular brooch. The circle was made from a strip of metal, cut and bent, then hammered to make a concave shape. The pin is of 14 carat pink gold, with the garnet held in the end that slips around the circle. The "tree", fashioned by use of mokumé gané, has a forged trunk, which is soldered to the other end of the ring.

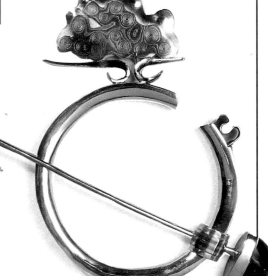

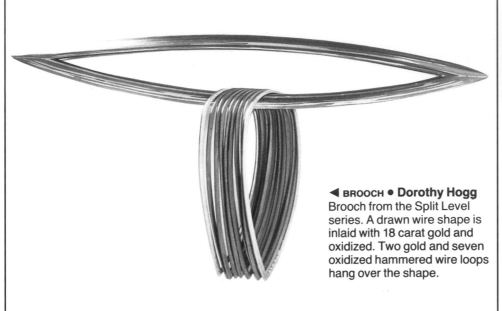

◀ BROOCH ● **Dorothy Hogg**
Brooch from the Split Level series. A drawn wire shape is inlaid with 18 carat gold and oxidized. Two gold and seven oxidized hammered wire loops hang over the shape.

▶ RED EARTH ● **Trevor Jennings**
A fabricated piece made from bronze sheet. The natural surface patination is a result of the heat processes of construction. It measures 7cm (2¾in) in diameter.

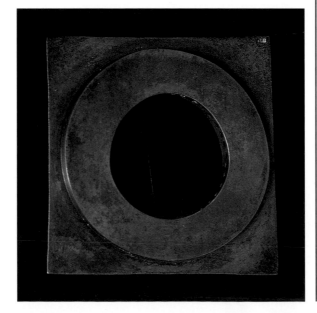

▲ AMPHORA CU 1 ● **Susan Kingsley**
This piece measures 90 x 40 x 20mm (3½ x 1½ x ¾in). It consists of a small, hollow pendant, made of copper, which is held on a leather cord. The two halves of the miniature amphora were formed in a hydraulic press, then the separate pieces were shaped in matrix dies before being soldered together. Finally, the copper was coloured with patinas.

▶ **BROOCHES AND EARRINGS** ●
Debby Moxon
This selection of jewellery was made from heat-treated sheet titanium and white metal. The designer drew the patterns with a ruler and scribe and then used heat to apply the colours, starting with the hottest tones and using a flux solution to mask the other areas. When the first colour had been successfully applied, the flux was removed with sulphuric acid and the area cleaned with emery papers. The process was then repeated at a lower temperature to apply the next colour.

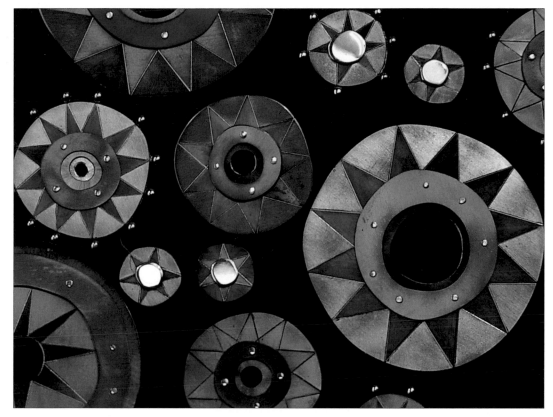

◀ **BROOCH** ● **Patricia McAnally**
This piece is made from sterling silver and 18 and 24 carat gold with a tourmaline, using roller texturring, press moulding and reticulation. The decoration has been soldered.

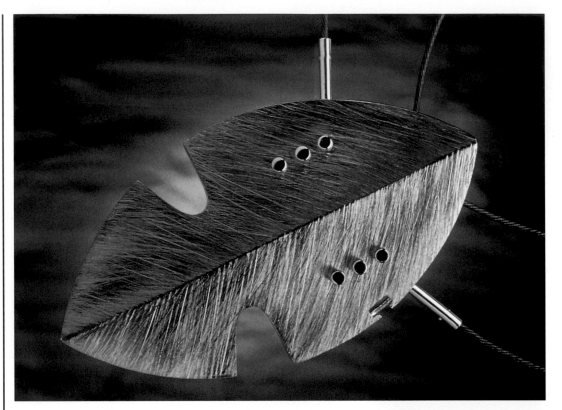

◀ PENDANT ● Boris Bally
This pendant was made in the shape of a Zulu shield. The centrepiece is of fabricated sterling silver, the texture on the front was created using a coarse checkering file and then burnished. The six central circular elements are decorative rivet tubes. The secure twisted steel cable is also riveted.

▶ RING ● Elke Storch
An 18 carat yellow and white gold ring set with a single diamond. The decoration was created by reticulation.

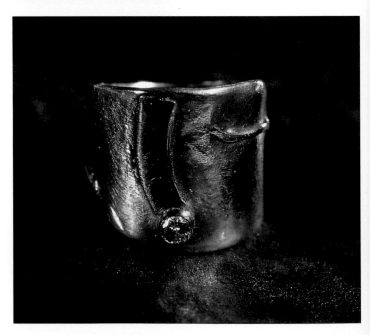

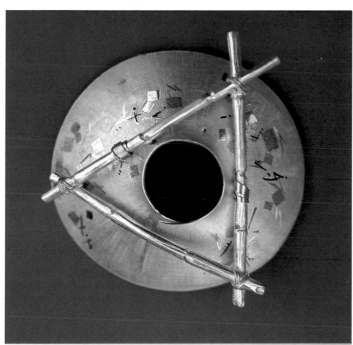

◀ BRACELET • **Jacqueline Mina**
This measures 6.3cm (2½in) deep and with a diameter of 6.3cm (2½in), made of partly oxidized 18 carat yellow gold with a platinum ganza fusion inlay.

▶ BROOCH • **Philippa Crawford**
This was made from a sheet of copper, which was rubbed down to give it a texture before chemicals and paints were applied to alter the surface. A resist was applied and the surface scratched before further coats of chemicals and paints were applied, with the process being repeated until the designer achieved the desired result.

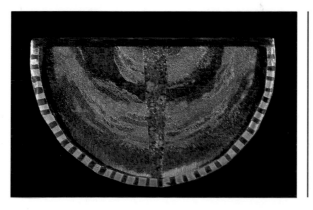

▲ JAPAN-MOTIFS #1 • **Lynda Watson-Abbott**
This brooch is made of fine and sterling silver and 24 carat gold. It measures 70 x 76 x 12mm (2¾ x 3 x ½in). The surface of the fine silver sheet was textured with a roulette and the separate sections were burnished.

153

Stones

The jewellery illustrated on the following pages are pieces that have been made with the colour of the stone as their central feature. The metal is used to enhance the stone rather than being allowed to take centre stage in its own right.

It is a constant source of amazement that so many different colours and qualities are formed deep within the earth. Whether you use them singly or in groups, it is important to consider the combination very carefully – some jewels look wonderful together while other combinations seem to look dead and unappealing. The examples illustrated will show how stunning a simple stone can be when it is used in a sympathetic way – either with another stone or group of stones or with an attractively textured metal or in an unusual setting. Although some pieces may look as if they have been made from a random selection of materials, the very simplicity belies the care with which the different components have been used together.

Precious stones are not cheap. Always obtain your supplies through a reputable dealer and make the most of them, using each one in a carefully thought out and executed design.

Among the semi-precious stones that are popular with jewellery makers are the wonderfully lined moss agate, magical amber and shimmering mystery of moonstones. And these stones are so reasonably priced that they offer opportunities to experiment with new techniques and designs.

Stones do not have to be precious or even semi-precious. Even everyday stones are so tactile and coolly beautiful when they are cut, set and polished that they can never fail to inspire us to find ways to share their beauty.

▲ BROOCH ● **Charmian Harris**
The background was created by reticulating the silver. The designer then pierced out the motifs from silver, brass and copper by hand. The motifs were textured by stamping, and they were soldered to the background before the stone was set.

▲ BROOCH ● **Fred Rich**
This is a chased 18 carat gold enamel and amethyst brooch. Cloisonné and basse taille enamel have been used.

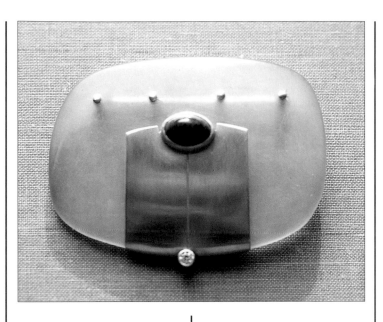

◄ BROOCH • **Klaus Kallenberger**
A brooch made of lexan (a type of plastic), sterling silver, sugulite and cubic zirconia. The silver was riveted to the lightly sanded lexan, and the stones were bezel set.

▼ EARRINGS • **Fred Rich**
The designer chased 18 carat yellow and white gold to make the backing for the multicoloured cloisonné enamel. The cloisonné pieces were then attached to the set amethysts.

▼ BROOCH • **Stephen Maer**
This silver and amethyst brooch has a free-form textured surface design produced by repoussé. The frosted finish is achieved by immersion in sulphuric acid and left unpolished. Edges are highly polished to provide contrast and define the outline. A cabochon amethyst is set on a stalk in a rub-over (bezel) setting.

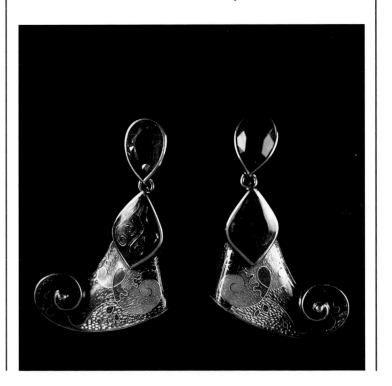

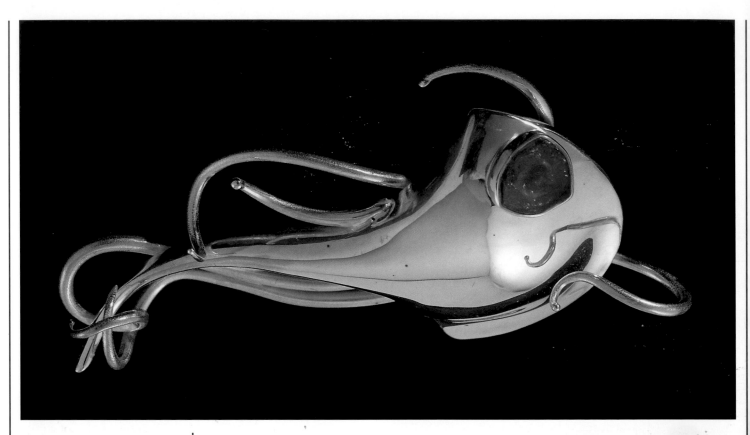

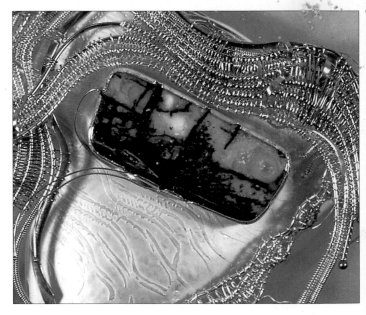

▲ PIN ● **Michael and Maureen Banner**
The designers used sterling silver and tourmaline crystal to make this pin. The main part of the brooch was formed and fabricated from a sheet of silver, and the tendrils were forged. The stone was bezel mounted, and when it was finished the whole piece was highly polished.

► BROOCH ● **Barbara Patrick**
This delicate brooch was made from fine silver, sterling silver and pink, yellow and green 14, 18 and 22 carat gold. The piece was twined, photoetched and forged before the Australian opal and pearl were set.

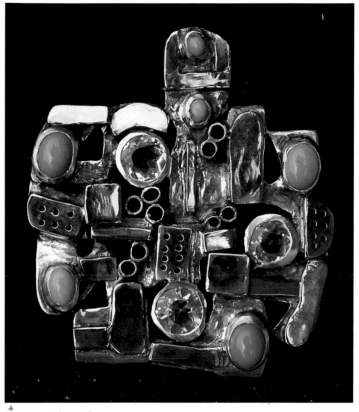

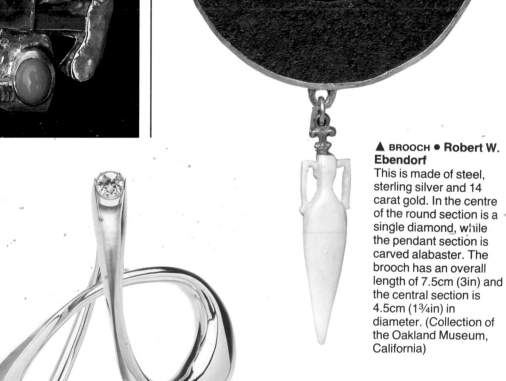

▲ MOON LANDSCAPE ● Resia Schor
This pendant is made of silver and 14 carat gold with turquoise and aquamarine stones. The metals were cut out and assembled by soldering before being oxidized and polished.

▶ BROOCH ● Liz Tyler
This 18 carat yellow gold brooch has been set with three 1 carat, brilliant cut diamonds. The designer raised the brooch from one sheet of fine-gauge metal using the anticlastic raising technique so that the two curves were formed in opposite directions. The diamond settings were soldered when the brooch was complete.

▲ BROOCH ● Robert W. Ebendorf
This is made of steel, sterling silver and 14 carat gold. In the centre of the round section is a single diamond, while the pendant section is carved alabaster. The brooch has an overall length of 7.5cm (3in) and the central section is 4.5cm (1¾in) in diameter. (Collection of the Oakland Museum, California)

▲ **ANCIENT FUTURE #2** ●
James Barker
This necklace is made from a combination of 18 and 22 carat golds and has been entirely fabricated by hand. The stones are positioned in a random pattern to accentuate their different colours and forms.

▶ **THE OPERA OF DREAMS** ●
James Barker
Diamonds have been used with faceted, sliced and cabochon tourmalines, and they have all been set on a series of linked units. A combination of 18 and 22 carat golds was used.

▲ NECKLACE • **James Barker**
The central feature on this pendant is a large Mabé pearl and it is accompanied by 83 carats' worth of diamonds. This piece holds the Award of Honorable Mention from the 1994 International Pearl Design Contest.

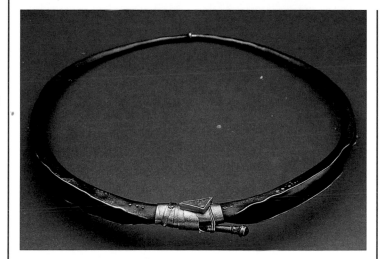

▲ NECKPIECE • **Andrew Cooperman**
From the "Bandage" series. This necklace was reticulated, formed and fabricated. It is made from 14 and 18 carat gold with bronze, cobocalcite, citrine and ruby.

▲ KRESIVE ENSIS II • **Rebecca Reimers Cristol**
This pendant is made of sterling silver, 18 carat gold, 22 carat gold and fluorite. The pendant was cast and the stone was hand carved. The hand-made chain is 75cm (30in) long and the pendant itself is 5cm (2in) long.

► NECKLACE • **Anna Tortorelli**
This 18 carat gold necklace was formed by piercing, milling and soldering. When the metal was shaped and finished, the blue glass was fused into the fold.

► NURTURE • **Rebecca Reimers Cristol**
A detail of a pendant made of fine silver, sterling silver, 10, 14, 18 and 22 carat gold with a hard-carved ruby, which measures 50 x 40 x 5mm (2 x 1½ x ¼in). The Roman-style chain, which is 75cm (30in) long, is a hand-woven, loop-in-loop chain.

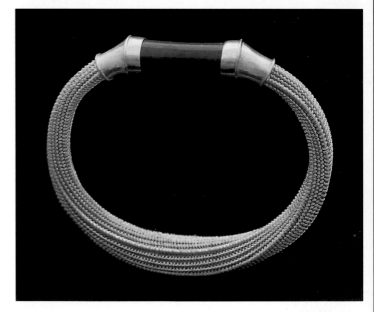

◄ PENDANT • **David Hensel**
This striking pendant is made of carved rock crystal (quartz), silver and gold with opals and garnet. The metals were made to fit the rock crystal by the lost wax casting method.

▲ BRACELET • **Mary Lee Hu**
In this piece, the 18 carat gold is used for the warp and bezel on the edge, whilst the 22 carat gold is used for weaving (twining). Unusually, the designer has used a double weft as opposed to the more common single weft. The inset bar is made from a single piece of lapis lazuli bezel set from both ends.

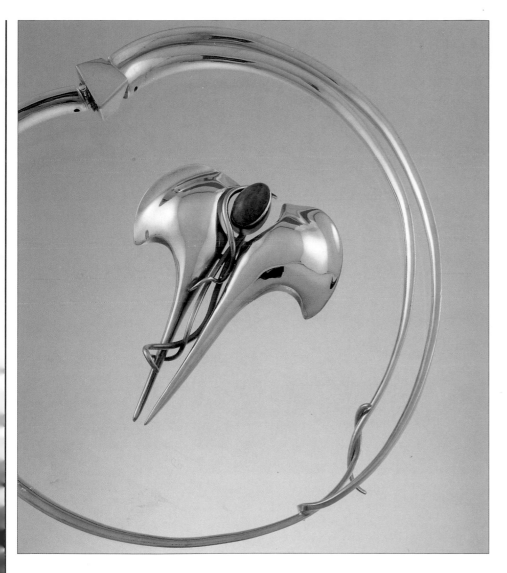

◀ **PIN AND NECK COLLAR ●**
Michael and Maureen Banner
This unusual pin with a
labradorite stone and the neck
collar, of which a detail is
shown, are made of sterling
silver. The pieces were hollow
formed and fabricated from
sheet metal before being highly
polished. The neck collar has a
tension hinge and the stone in
the pin is bezel mounted. The
tendrils on the pin were forged.

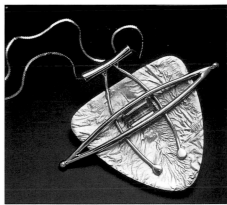

▲ **PENDANT ● Rebecca**
Reimers Cristol
A pendant made from 14 carat
gold, with a cleverly designed
setting for the ametrine.

▶ **BROOCHES ● Gun Thor**
The brooches were cast in
silver, then filed, cleaned and
sandpapered to give them a
perfectly smooth finish. Bezels
and brooch fittings were
soldered on, and the pieces
were buffed again. The stones
were set in position and pins
riveted to the backs. A final
polishing gave the silver a satin-
smooth finish.

▲ EARRINGS ● Robert W. Ebendorf
These were made in 14 carat gold with pearls, iron and beach glass and, at centre top, a turquoise. Each earring is 6.5cm (2½in) long.

◄ EARRINGS ● Stephen Webster
These 18 carat gold earrings, which were inspired by paisley designs, are set with amethysts, 0.8 carat diamonds and South Sea pearl drops.

▼ DIAL EARRINGS ● Elizabeth Maldonado
These are made of sterling silver, 18 carat gold, semi-precious stones (blue agate and garnet) and applied non-vitreous metal. Small photoetched triangles were soldered to the main flat, round body, which were formed from discs no more than 1.4mm thick. Other shapes, including the wire and gold setting and the round cup for the central stones, were soldered into position. The metal was polished before the stones were inserted and, finally, the cold (non-vitreous) enamel was applied. The hallmarks have been used as an integral feature of the design.

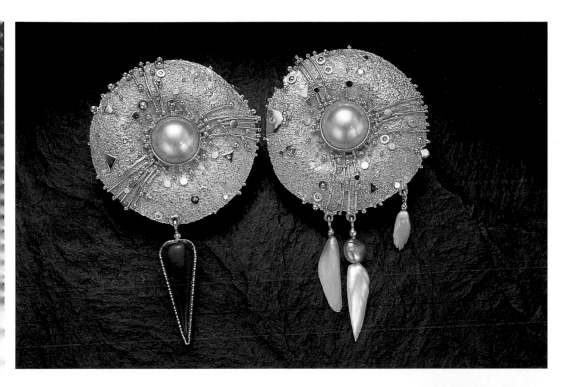

◄ EARRINGS ● **James Barker**
The purple stone used here is a sugilite, along with Mabé pearls in the centre of the discs and natural American freshwater pearls for the drops. The omega backings are located at the back, at the point corresponding to the top edge of the pearl.

◄ EARRINGS ● **James Barker**
No casting was used to make these earrings set with Mabé pearls and diamonds. Fine gauge 22 carat wire balls were inlayed into the central pearl. The design was partly inspired by the patterns found in African basketweaving.

▲ EARRINGS ● Robert W. Ebendorf
One of a pair of earrings made in 14 carat gold with pearls, lead iron and beach glass and, at centre top, a turquoise. Each earring is 6.5cm (2½in) long.

◄ NATURALLY DIVINE ● Ben Dyer
A pair of earrings made from fabricated 18 and 22 carat gold with azurite, boulder Australian opals, pearls and diamonds. Each earring is 20 x 65mm (¾ x 2½in).

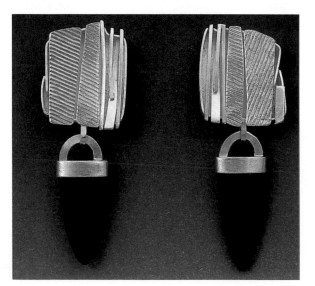

▲ EARRINGS ● Barbara Patrick
The designer set chrysophase and conicalcite in 14, 18 and 22 carat yellow and red gold. Photoetching was used to transfer the decoration onto the metal.

◄ EARRINGS ● Micki Lippe
Sterling silver and 22 carat gold were combined to make this pair of earrings. The dramatic drop is black onyx.

This is crafted from 18 carat yellow gold and set with labradorite. The surface of the gold has been subtly reticulated.

Mixed Media

When it comes to making the pieces illustrated in this section, anything goes! Any colours, materials or textures can be combined to make some really fascinating pieces of jewellery.

Using material with only little intrinsic value offers opportunities, not always available with more valuable metals and stones, to give your imagination full rein. Experiment with both traditional and a range of non-traditional jewellery making techniques to produce unusual but wearable items. What could be more fun than picking up odd pieces of wood, plastic, tin, glass, bone and fabric, and transforming them by cutting, shaping, painting, carving and gluing them in different ways.

As you will see from the pieces illustrated on the pages that follow, skilled designers and jewellery makers use a range of manmade materials – including pieces of plastic, perspex, PVC, resin and acrylic – and combine them with *objets trouvés* such as shells and pebbles and even handmade paper, postage stamps and photographs to make some wonderfully inventive and attractive pieces. Look around your home for unusual articles that you might be able to incorporate into your work – this is a good way of recycling bits of plastic – and try working with modelling clay, which is available in a wide range of colours and can be easily moulded and shaped.

Some of these articles of jewellery are made with silver and gold, although you should note that very few pieces of mixed media jewellery can be hallmarked. However, metals such as copper and even stainless steel can be used, and mixed media jewellery offers a wonderful opportunity to use metals such as titanium and niobium, which you might not otherwise think of using.

Even if your first efforts are not altogether successful, you will have a lot of fun stretching your jewellery making techniques – and your imagination – to the full.

▲ **PIN FOR A SHAMAN ● Alice Vandewetering**
This brooch is 9cm (3½in) across. It is made of sterling silver, and the little amulets suspended from the bottom edge are of clay, fossil, horn, stone, and amber and wood beads. The techniques used included piercing, soldering, reticulating and applying a liver of sulphur patina.

▲ **BROOCH ● Edward Williams**
The designer used wood-carving tools to cut and then carve the design into a sheet of ebony. The silver backplate was attached to the ebony by pins, which were inserted into glue-filled holes drilled into the wood. Silver balls were soldered to the main sheet. The small loops along the bottom were created by heating wire and wrapping it around a knitting needle. Each loop was cut with a piercing saw, cooled and then soldered to the silver. After each soldering, the sheet was dipped into a boiling solution of alum and water.

▶ **EARRINGS AND BROOCH** ●
Amy Sabrina
These earrings, 2.5cm (1in) long, and the matching brooch 4 x 3cm (1½ x 1¼in), are decorated with food and kitchen-related motifs. The earthenware clay was rolled and cut to shape before being hand painted, glazed and fired. Little onyx beads were threaded onto the silver wire ear hoops.

▼ **SHIM BRACELET #2** ● **Susan Hamlet**
The very thin stainless steel shim was formed on a rotary combination machine, and the other metal and plastic elements are secured to it by means of custom-made screws and nuts. The black rim is a rubber tube, cut open and glued in place.

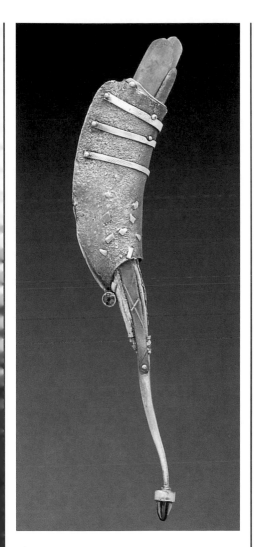

▲ **ICE MAN #2** ●
A. Cooperman
This brooch measures 11 x 5cm (4½ x 2in). It is made of 14 and 18 carat gold and shibuichi, citrine, ruby and sea urchin spines. The surface of the metal was torch-textured and the overall shape was forged and fabricated.

▶ **SQUIG** • **Debra Lynn Gold**
These earrings are made of coloured aluminium, sterling silver and vinyl. The aluminium was hand-engraved and then coloured. After it was fabricated, the pieces were held with sterling silver rivets and sterling silver ear wires were added. Each earring measures 9 x 4 x 3cm (3½ x 1½ x 1¼in).

▼ **BROOCHES AND EARRINGS** •
Rowena Park
Inspired by images at the fairground, the designer used clear acrylic, which was engraved, inlaid, shaped, polished and painted to create these pieces.

▲ **BROOCH AND EARRINGS** •
Anne Finlay
For these, geometric patterns were screenprinted on to PVC sheet, then shapes were cut out using an engraving machine, or by hand using a scalpel and template. These shapes were combined with dyed nylon, rubber and stainless steel wire, by drilling, bonding and other simple assembly techniques.

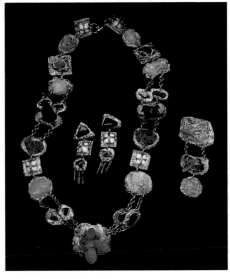

▲ MINER'S DREAM • **Pauletta Brooks**
This is a necklace, earrings and brooch set, in which all the pieces were sculpted from thermoplastic resin mesh. The necklace is made of quartz, garnet, ivory, irradiated quartz and a fossil shell on an antique brass chain. Each earring is formed from a fossil shell, ivory, jasper drops and faux pearls on a 14 carat gold post. The brooch contains bornite, quartz and irradiated quartz.

▲ LOST AND FOUND • **Robert W. Ebendorf**
This whimsical arrangement of items into a necklace is made of mixed media, including wood and iron. The whole piece is 25cm (10in) in diameter.

◄ BRACELET • **Avrina Eggleston**
The basic piece was made from sheet silver, with hinges made from lengths of chenier. The granulations are from gold. The gem settings were worked from sheet metal, while the elephant and Buddha were cast by the cuttlefish method. The doors and other details are enamel, while the safety chain is twisted yellow gold wire. The palm trees at the back of the links were drilled and sawed out.

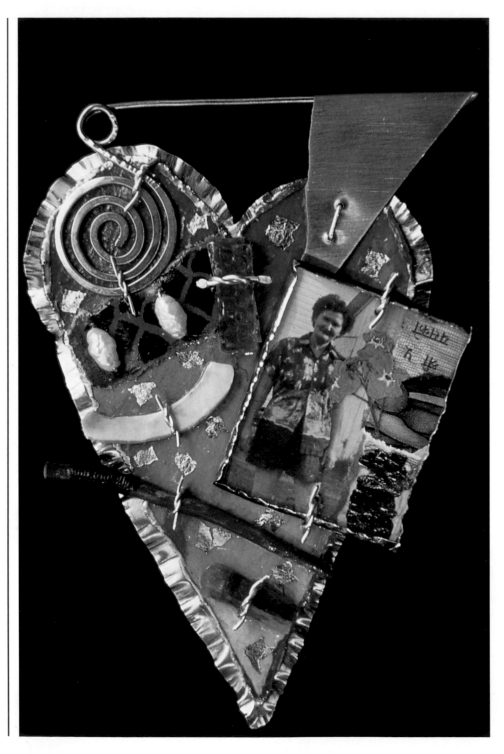

Ken Bova
This brooch measures 8.5 x 6.5cm (3⅜ x 2⅝in). It is made of 14 and 23 carat gold, sterling silver, fine silver, paper, pastel, tourmaline, pearls, bone, wood, silk, a photograph, a flower and a plastic reflector. The designer used no glue in assembling the elements of the composition, but relied instead on riveting, scoring, folding, tying, hammering, wrapping, stamping and bolting.

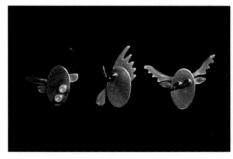

▲ TIE PINS ● **Brigitte Turba**
These tie pins are made from toothbrush handles that have been sawn out, filed, sanded and polished. The silver is hollow and the edges are soldered together.

▲ **EMBROIDERED JEWELLERY** ●
Janice Gilmore
These earrings and brooches
were made by both machine
and hand-stitching techniques
using threads, silk and fine
beads.

▲ **HAIR SLIDE Sammie Bell**
This witty hair slide has been
created using the decorative
faces and mechanisms of both
pocket and wrist watches.

▶ **NECKLACE** ● **Robert W.
Ebendorf**
Among the media used to
create this piece were a sea
shell, bone, gold foil, blue cut
glass, beach pebbles, slate, old
photographs, postage stamps,
formica, Japanese handmade
paper and niobium.

▶ **EARRINGS AND BROOCH** ●
Rowena Park
The design for these earrings was inspired by quartz, using clear acrylic that was engraved, inlaid, shaped, polished and painted.

◀ **BANGLES** ● **Helen Sloan**
These three resin bangles were made from clear casting polyester resin, ordinary cold water dyes and soft solder. The resin was cast in latex moulds, and the silver-coloured nuggets, which are made from soft solder, were embedded in clear resin. Green chips were cut from jelled resin and suspended in liquid resin. To give an uneven colour, dye was poured into slightly jelled liquid resin while it was still in the mould, and further modelling was achieved by filing and sanding. The bangles were finished in a barrelling machine.

◀ **BRACELET** • **Peter Chang**
This bracelet, which has an external diameter of 20cm (8in) and is 4.5cm (1¾in) thick, is made of polyester, acrylic and PVC. The GRP core has metal-reinforced spindles, which were built up with a variety of objects, including beads and pin heads, some of which were lathe-turned to give the required shapes. Some of the spokes are laminated and carved and some are inlaid with PVC.

▶ **EARRINGS** • **Ingrid Scheiffert**
Silver and perspex were used to make these earrings, which involved cutting, drilling, polishing and doming.

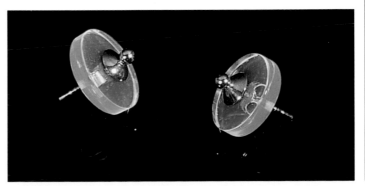

Index

Credits

The author and Quarto would like to thank all the jewellery makers who have kindly allowed us to reproduce their work in this book.

A special thanks to Bedales School in Hampshire for their very generous loan of their jewellery workshop.

My thanks also to all who helped with the project techniques: Penny Warren – patinating; Sarah Packington – acrylics; Naomi James – stamping and making blanks; Chris Hawkins – stone setting; and last but not least Jonathan Swan – anodizing and lots of tips.

We would also like to acknowledge the following photographers: page 140*bl* Brian Young; 140*r* Mark Thomason; 141*al* Graham Portlock; 142*r* Brian Young; 144*b*, 147*ar*, 149*al* Joel Degen; 150*ar* Lee Hocker; 151*b* Maggie Campbell Pedersen; 152*a* Dean Powell; 153*al* Joel Degen; 159*b* Douglas Yaple; 160*br* Richard Nicol; 164*b* Richard Nichol; 166*r* Ralph Gabriner; 167*l* Douglas Yaple; 169*al* P. Marus.
(Key: *a* above, *b* below, *l* left, *r* right)

We are indebted to H. S. Walsh & Sons Ltd, 15 Clerkenwell Road, London EC1M 5PL, who kindly loaned equipment for use in photography.

We would also like to thank the following for the loan of materials used in photography; Michael Bloomstein, of Bloomsteins, 30 Gloucester Road, Brighton, East Sussex BN1 4AQ (precious metals); Goodfellow Cambridge Ltd, Unit 204, Cambridge Science Park, Cambridge CB4 4DJ (metals); John Bell & Croyden, 50 Wigmore Street, London W1H 9DG (chemicals); and Marcia Lanyon Ltd, PO Box 370, London W6 7ED (precious and semi-precious stones). We would also like to thank Alexandra Raphael, who kindly loaned enamel.